WOMAN POWER:

THE MOVEMENT FOR WOMEN'S LIBERATION

Cellestine Ware

D1299897

A TOWER PUBLIC AFFAIRS BOOK

WOMAN POWER: THE MOVEMENT FOR
WOMEN'S LIBERATION

Copyright © 1970 by Cellestine Ware

Tower Publications, Inc.
185 Madison Avenue
New York, New York 10016

Goals . . .

Radical feminism is working for the eradication of domination and elitism in all human relationships. This would make self-determination the ultimate good and require the downfall of society as we know it today.

Contents

Preface

"I am too American myself and lack juices."
—Henry James

Throughout history there have been reorderings of "nature" whereby real changes in human sentiment, with a resultant difference in modes of conduct, have occurred. The renaissance of feminism seems part of such a phenomenon. The attempt in this preface to explain its causes are based on my scrutiny of the social and cultural environment in which it is occurring. Nevertheless, despite circumstantial explanations, the mystery of the resurgence of feminism in the end remains inviolate.

The rebirth of feminism is part of a change in sentiment that has developed along two axes: the desire for deep spiritual satisfaction and the attempt to model a society in which individuals can express and activate all their capacities. Psychologically, America remained a frontier well into the twentieth century. Indeed, Frederick Jackson Turner constructed his entire theory of American history around this view. This was a frontier country long after the struggle to subdue nature was won. The extension of the frontier, empire-building, had been for so long the preoccupation of America that the thoughts and feelings appropriate to that concern continued to inform American consciousness until the 50's. The emotional organization of frontier America is typified in the western and, to a lesser degree, in the detective story. The strongest bond is the love of man

7

for man: the mutual regard and affection of men who live by a code and die together fighting odds. This American cultural tradition of heroic man conquering nature, first with the strength of his body, and then by the application of technology, runs throughout American literature and art.

By advancing the frontier, American men grew adept at changing the environment. True and interesting life came to mean defiant physical gestures, laconic speech and sparse emotional expression—the cool, dry style on which today's American men still pattern themselves. In the stories of Jack London and in Hemingway, up to and including the 1969 movie *Butch Cassidy and the Sundance Kid*, women are excluded from the mainstream of action and thought. The poverty of the male-female relationship is well exemplified in the movie *The Hustler*. The best scenes take place among the men because it is through the relationships of the men that psychological and socio-economic changes take place. Only men have power. Where this film is successful, it confirms the frontier organization of emotion and style of encountering life. The movie fails whenever it tries to include the woman in the interchanges between the protagonists. Love of women suggests loss of control, which is antithetical to the continual reassertion of manhood that the frontier demands and stimulates.

Essentially then, in frontier America, experience was transformed to fit the truncated self-image of the strong, silent frontiersman. The wellspring of passion and sensibility seemed dried up in this grim process. The politics of the country reflected back this image of the good man. America had Lincoln and Wilson, while Europe had Disraeli and Clemenceau. The result was that Americans felt they had to go to Europe to learn aesthesia. Europe was a woman of experience: supersensual, spiritual, mystic. The necessity of going abroad was felt by Americans from Henry James, through the

8

"lost generation" of post WW I, to the intellectuals and artists who returned to Europe after WW II.

The quest, whose purpose was the return to white America of life, wonder and richness in artistic imagery and which eventuated in the rebirth of feminism, first became evident in the 50's. The collegians of that era were dubbed "the silent generation," and the women of the time were a silent, although restless, majority. It has been pointed out that this was the period in which many of the best minds of a generation were carried off to the suburbs and kept there very well. However, there were bohemian ghettos on the east and west coasts where a new kind of emotive existence was possible.

The generation of whites who grew up in America during the Depression and WW II included only a tiny group of people who lived beyond and above the frontier. Their idols were the people "who laid down the patterns of extreme beauty for this civilization." Transcribed from these idols, the existential living of the 50's and very early 60's was a taking to the road to seek out uncontrollable events that would engulf the seekers in feelings and reactions. The Few sought out those experiences described by Norman Mailer: "When violence is larger than one's ability to dominate it . . . and one is living in an instantaneous world of revelations." The result of these confrontations was the difference between *Howl* and *The Waste Land,* or, on a different level, between *The Sun Also Rises* and *Lolita,* which is possibly the ultimate expression of the road novel.

Fluency in the expression of feeling already existed in America before the Beats made their journey to the interior. There had been all along in America a population that had been deliberately refused a share of the power accrued through the exploitation of American resources. This population had helped to build the frontier but had been excluded from frontier society. Here I do not mean American white women—although the description might fit them too. The black community and its art forms constituted a separate ethos with

9

a contextual richness and authenticity that was deep, thrilling and moving: the result of a luxuriant emotionality not unlike that relegated to women, a style that was the mirror image of the western hero's stolidity. The whites of the 50's, recognizing the power of this art and drawn to the glamor personified by its practitioners, began consciously to mimic the life-style of the black subculture. These people, followers of blues and jazz life, which is the cult of experience and existentialism American-style, were the most obvious explorers of inner space in the 50's. The mystique of the blues life is that oppression gives knowledge by distancing the oppressed from common reality. This is that same distance that American innocents traveled to Europe to achieve. Suffering is seen as a kind of artistry. Blues and jazz music are the precipitates, the emotional and artistic expressions of this life.

That the ability to feel deeply and give artistic expression to a freely ranging emotionality are part of the mystique of black music to this day is shown by the following quotation from a recent review in *The Village Voice*: "Never ask a jazz singer about her life. If she is any good, you will know all the answers by the time she steps offstage." Thus, the recognition came that the conditions for the fluent expression of feeling already existed in America among the classless and could be experienced in violent confrontations with reality.

The formal change that the beatific generation made in patterns of relationships in America was the establishment of the reality of small groups and of emotional and intellectual interchanges within them. This was the result of the coordination of the artists and intellectuals of the 50's into a series of cabals that was an identifying characteristic of that time.

In the 50's, the beatific few became legion as experimentation with drugs to achieve transcendental states of consciousness, and thereby kill one's conditioning, became widespread. The new *Rimbaldiens* disordered the mind with drugs in the belief that hallucinatory states free the spirit to explore otherwise intangible truths. As the decade evolved, the search for spiritual truth and a society congenial to self-actualization took many forms, but its purpose was always the same.

The habit of questioning institutional behavior (Does this institution or custom allow me to live "in a way that is deeply satisfying to me and which truly expresses me?") was acquired by the generation that came of age in the 60's, and radicalization of consciousness is a one-way street. Many of the people who would have been beatniks in the 50's turned, in the 60's, to political action to create the possibility of self-actualization for everybody (campaigning for black civil rights in the South was certainly existential living).

The sit-ins and freedom rides brought to the surface the racism and intolerance of America. In learning to deal with increasingly violent confrontations, blacks developed their capacity for aggression, self-assertion and the expression of rage. Mao replaced Gandhi at the universities. Blacks and whites realized that white people were irrelevant to the black struggle, which became essentially a demand for self-determination and the right to develop a truly black identity and organization of energy. Stokely Carmichael's message to white radicals was to look to their own oppression. This admonition was one of the inspirations of the new feminist movement as we shall see. Black Is Beautiful is the direct antecedent to Women Are People.

The radicals were displaced from the black struggle, but Tom Hayden was to visit North Vietnam that year (1967) and would return to coordinate students protesting that education was a form of social control rather than a guide to self-realization. Eventually these protestants would find themselves with the same enemies as the critics and demonstrators against the war in Vietnam. The complaint was the same. Society was forcing people to present abbreviated versions of themselves in order to fulfil the needs of the established order.

11

Many of these white American protestants, displaced from the Great Society, went to California with flowers in their hair and there found the celebration of a new way of being and relating to others. Their *assumption* of freedom through living and dressing so differently from middle-class America and their attempts to slough off the middle-class character was a political act, although unorganized.

Through the magic of the media this experience has been carried throughout America and destroyed, for that is the new American way of death. Ralph Gleason's description of the Saturday afternoon crowd at the first "Human Be-In" as "benign" (imagine a benign western hero!) foreshadows Al Aronowitz's description of Woodstock as the "benign monster with the marijuana breath."

Americans proved as unable to tolerate the new mode of feeling as they had the non-violent demonstrations for civil rights, but the manner of suppressing it was less obviously deliberate—at the time. The country publicized Haight-Ashbury to death and commercialized the surface manifestations of that community.

But the melody lingers on. A generation had discovered that deep feeling and spontaneity were delightful. The first "Human Be-In" or "Gathering of the Tribes" in January, 1967, at San Francisco's Golden Gate Park was described by Ralph Gleason as "a remarkable event, the kind which grows in retrospect and assumes the nature of a mystical, religious happening." (Remember happenings?) "Mystical, religious happening" are the key words here. The affirmation of pleasure in nature and sensuous experiences, of tolerance for every form of self-expression, was the first visible mass expression of a new way of feeling and being. The last frontier of non-feeling had been breached.

For a while in the 60's the two developments, radical activism and the feel-yourself orientation, were at opposite poles, but people like Peter Berg and Peter

12

Cohon, founding members of the S.F. Mime Troupe and the Diggers and creators of street or guerrilla theatre, seemed to fuse both organizations of energy. (The Yippies appear to be direct descendants of the Berg-Cohon synthesis.) This fusion was an important base for the new feminism.

People moved toward this fusion from two different directions: the countercultural sensibility and the New Left. Once they came together, the politics of immediacy declared everyone's right to do his own thing. Drugs are a means of achieving the new sensibility. Drugs offer a way out from under the weight of the middle-class personality. Drugs are a substitution for the oppression and brutalization of blackness, poverty and illegitimacy. H. Rap Brown said: "White kids take heroin as a short-cut to soul." "Drugs are hard kicks, and hard kicks are a way of acquiring life." (Peter Berg).

A cross-pollination of life-styles occurred in the late 60's. The hybrid result was the politics of experience. The impetus to drop out of non-feeling, plastic, uptight America overlapped with the demand for the right to determine the quality of life in the society the protestants inhabited. The new sensibility informed the search for a politics as well. The most recent march in Washington to protest the war in Vietnam was called "Woodstock South" and "Berkeley East."

The dropouts wanted out of the privatism of the 50's: out of the insularity of the middle-class suburbs. The new religion was communication—with your self and with others. The children of the electronic age wanted to feel the cosmic energies and vibrate in harmony with nature and each person encountered. Sensitivity to vibrations and being out front became the ultimate good. "The life I am trying to grasp is the me that is trying to grasp it . . . If I could turn you on, if I could drive you out of your wretched mind, if I could tell you I would let you know," wrote R. D. Laing, British psychiatrist and guru.[1] Dr. Laing believes that the roles enforced by society have estranged humanity from its authentic possibilities, and this belief is basic to the new politics.

The meaning of politics has been expanded. Politics is the stuff that roles are made of. The old witticism that defines politics as the art of the possible speaks too much of the manipulation perpetrated daily by families, schools, businesses, the media, and the government. Confronting reality now means dropping indifference to others; it means stretching yourself to allow others living space. As the Beatles sang, "I am he as you are he as you are me, and we are all together," a togetherness righteously different from that of the Eisenhowever years. Still it remained a togetherness of men. Men in their political groups and men in their communes with women as their helpers.

Any description or definition of a new sensibility must coarsen it in the process of verbalizing it. For the first time political systems are being developed that validate the demand for happiness. Do your own thing is an inaccurate popularization of the new extensions of feeling and tolerance.

The new mental receptivity and readiness of discernment have come together with the demand for a right conduct. "Capacities are also needs" is the motto of the new season. The Women's Liberation Movement has the most revolutionary platform of any group in the new politics. The politics of women's liberation grows out of the study of the sociology of women's unhappiness and centers on finding the political solution to the dehumanizing role assigned women by society. Do your own thing translated into feminism is the demand for self-determination. The self-realization of feminism is analogous to the hippies' determination to be "out front," and is matched by the black militant's use of "righteous" and "right on" to denote authentic action. The Weatherman faction of SDS seeks to identify and implement "correct" work. Everywhere people are seeking a natural order through which they can become themselves.

14

The feminist dictum that every woman can testify to the truth of her sex-class oppression, the Weatherman romanticization of people and the Black Panther saying that "the spirit of the people is always greater than the man's technology," are parallel expressions of the unfeeling, unradicalized consciousness. The new enthusiasm for encounter groups and sensitivity training are manifestations of the same orientation. The *Zeitgeist* that expressed itself in the cabalism of the Beats is now manifesting itself in the hippie communes, the betogethers at Woodstock, Berkeley and Washington, the law communes to defend the new politicians, the group effort that puts out Liberation News Service and the underground press, and the collectives of the new feminists.

Chapter 1

The Politics of Women's Liberation

The Women's Liberation Movement can be seen as the logical extension of the insight that the pace and texture of life in America has become unresponsive to the dimensions and capacities of its people. This self-realization is to be distinguished from the concept of individualism, which many radical feminists see as a possible stumbling block, particularly because of the media attention the movement is receiving. Radical feminists are not interested in creating famous women: The avowed purpose of their revolution is a society in "which you don't have to be famous to be heard." Radical feminism, and this by no means includes all positions within the Women's Liberation Movement, postulates that the domination of one human by another is the basic evil in society. Dominance in human relationships is the target of their opposition. The doctrine of untrammeled being is an idea whose time has come.

"Look to your own oppression." When the New Left women appraised their situation, they discovered that their exploitation and depersonalization within radical society was much the same as that of blacks and oppressed groups everywhere.

Make love, not war is great for men, but at Woodstock this was translated into, "Why don't some of you girls donate your bodies?" Women turned stroboscopic eyes on the selves they had introjected to discover that women, as they exist in society, are the creatures of men. Women activists came full circle in the shock of recognizing that they had been the house niggers in the New Left.

Kick out the jams doesn't apply to the jelly roll. Until now, radical analysis has always stopped short of male domination of the female. Within the various movements that women joined to alter the quality of life in America, they found themselves betrayed. Again and again they were forced to play peahens to the peacocks, administresses to the agonists, handmaidens to the lords. This feminist understanding, which had slipped from memory in the years since the struggle for suffrage, knew again the male view that women are automatically outsiders, the necessary evil.

At the national SDS convention in the summer of 1967, a women's caucus read a Women's Manifesto. SDS was praised at the time for taking recognition of the fact that women lacked a voice in the leadership of the party. The recognition was a purely formal one. The liberation of women—SDS is said to have coined the phrase—was an issue considered irrelevant to the struggle. At that, the women's list of grievances seems to have been written without insight into the nature of their oppression and without an attempt to devise a new logic and rhetoric for the description of their injustices. The Manifesto, constantly employing the language of the New Left, makes ready references to capitalism, socialism and Third World politics, all of which were illogically assumed to be proper sources for women's fight against oppression.

Feminism, having died after the passage of the 19th Amendment, arose again in the late 60's to proclaim self-determination the ultimate good. Each person is to occupy that space in this world which has been self-described, and the feminist movement, with varying degrees of intensity, is organizing itself to combat the obstacles to this actuality.

When women finally gained the self-respect to consider their unhappiness a political issue, they began to deny that the ability to have children is the sum of a woman's capacities and needs. Childbearing is too confining a role for the extended electronic woman.

Women demanded that they be included back in the human race. The restless housewife, the radical activist, the student going out into the business world all found themselves, upon self-examination, to be oppressed in every aspect of their lives, condemned by their sex to the rigid confines of femininity.

Since 1963, feminism has again become a nationwide movement. There are women's liberation groups in every major city in the continental United States. Feminists are also active again in Canada and England. The movement is being buried under newsprint, but few of the people who have written on the subject seem to have comprehended that this is a political movement with a clearly traceable descent from the radical philosophies and politics of our time.

The reason for this failure to recognize feminism as a political movement is the novelty of the idea that discontent with social roles is the stuff of politics. Radical thinker Peter Cohon knows better: "To live an alternative that is totally outside the alternatives of this culture is a profoundly political act." For women, self-assertion is a political act. They have already become aware that privatism is a trap. Salvation through personal relationships, family and or religious experience will not change the constraining nature of the sociological identity of women. It still leaves each generation of women to fight as best it can the oppressive roles, character traits and abilities assigned women before they can begin to live in their own reality.

It was in Chicago in the summer of 1967 that the first new feminist group in the United States that hadn't originated as a caucus of a male organization was formed. The women who began the group, whose activator was Joreen Freeman, were wives or companions of the men who had come to Chicago to make that city the center of the radical movement in America.

Chicago had been chosen because it seemed to radicals to possess several elements necessary to catalyze a radical movement. The city is infamous for its corrupt

18

government, which makes few concessions to the needs of the large black ghetto that migrated to Chicago beginning with ww II. The city had no liberal or radical tradition. The political machine enjoyed great success in controlling the large immigrant European working-class population through manipulation of their fear and hatred of the blacks. Radical politicans felt that all the elements necessary for a revolutionary movement were present in Chicago in discrete, unorganized form.

When the women's group first started, its language and ideology were strongly influenced by the politics of the male left. The purpose of the group was the liberation of women, much as the liberation of the blacks, the poor and of the workers was the object of the New Left. The idea was to organize and liberate women *so that they could work for the eradication of oppressive elements in society*. This is the forerunner of the women radicals or "politico" faction in the feminist movement, typified by such organizations as Boston's BREAD AND ROSES and Berkeley's Women's Liberation Group. Most of the women in the group were married and felt threatened by radical analysis of the institutions of women's oppression, e.g., marriage.

Following what has come to seem the developmental norm for feminist groups, the Chicago group has since given women's issues top priority, although feminism is still not their sole concern. In this, too, it is like other New Left-oriented groups.

Founding members of the movement in Chicago were Joreen Freeman, Naomi Weisstein and Heather Booth. Heather was studying at the University of Chicago when the WOMEN'S RADICAL ACTION PROJECT (WRAP), a collective of women who were SDS dropouts, was formed. Heather Booth concentrates on abortion counseling, but she told an interviewer for *Mademoiselle* that "it's an organizing tool. These girls think their abortion is their personal problem, their shame. I tell them it's not—it's a problem in the structure of society. You know, *that's how you become a radical—when you realize a problem is societal, and not individual . . . when you start fighting your own battles."* (The italics in the preceding quote are mine because I think it is an excellent illustration of the fusion of radicalism with feminism.)

Judy Laws, an assistant professor of social psychology at the University of Chicago, was recently fired for wanting to do research on the sociology of women's oppression. She describes the evolution of a feminist from a woman radical. "That means I see the woman problem as the greatest neglected ill. I'm pessimistic about our impact on the war, and I'm convinced white people can't participate in the black movement, but I'm not a socialist, and I'm not a revolutionary, I mean— I wear a bra."

WL in Chicago has a Center where groups can meet and women can sleep when visiting Chicago. It is communal to the extent that the women take turns preparing meals, and share expenses. Joreen started the first WL newsletter at the 1967 National Convention of New Politics. Called *Voice of the Women's Liberation Movement,* it announced the liberation of women from their oppression as a problem as worthy of political struggle as any other that the New Politicians were considering.

Joreen has undergone an evolution since 1967. She told *Mademoiselle*: "The new people coming in now are more feminists than politicals. They care more about consciousness-raising than about organizing the worker."' Joreen might fairly have added that they care about radicalizing women and making demonstrations that raise women's consciousness of their societal oppression and reveal men to themselves as oppressors.

It was at the Chicago Convention for New Politics in 1967 that Shulamith Firestone, who had joined the Chicago women's groups in September of that year, met Pamela Allen. They decided to start a women's liberation group in New York. This was the duo that started the SCEF office meetings that were the beginning of the new feminism in New York.

In New York's feminist movement, there are no charismatic personalities. There are women who, by force of original thought or by vividness of personality, stand out from the others, but there is no one around whom all groups would rally. Moreover, many feminists are politically opposed to the development of famous spokeswomen.

In October, 1966, Betty Friedan, whose *The Feminine Mystique* (N. Y. 1963) pinpointed a national malaise, along with thirty-one other women and men from twelve states and Washington, D.C., organized NOW, the National Organization of Women. Unlike women's liberation organizations, NOW has male members.

NOW is reformist, works from within the system, and is referred to sometimes affectionately, sometimes impatiently as the forerunner of new feminism; and regarded much as black militants regard the civil rights organizations. The typical NOW member is middle class, employed full-time, and married.

By July, 1967, NOW had over a thousand members throughout the country. Today, its members total 5,000 in 50 chapters mostly in the cities of 24 states. Betty Friedan was the first national president. Their goal is "equal partnership with men."

This forerunner to the new feminism is efficiently and rigidly organized, rather like a business corporation. Businesslike, too, is the statement of purpose that was adopted by its organizing conference:

> We organize to initiate or support action, nationally, or in any part of this nation, by individuals or organizations, to break through the silken curtain of prejudice and discrimination against women, in government, industry, the professions, the churches, the political parties, the judiciary, the labor unions, in education, science, medicine, law, religion and every other field of importance in American society.

. . . Although 46.4% of all American women between the ages of 18 and 65 now work outside the home—the overwhelming majority—75%—are in routine clerical, sales or factory jobs, or they are household workers, cleaning women, hospital attendants. About two-thirds of Negro women workers are in the lowest paid service occupations. Working women are becoming increasingly—not less—concentrated on the bottom of the job ladder — . . . Full-time workers today earn on the average only 60% of what men earn . . . In 1964, of all women with a yearly income, 89% earned under $5,000 a year.

We are similarly opposed to all policies and practices—in church, state, college, or office—which, in the guise of protectiveness, not only deny opportunities but also foster in women self-denigration, dependence, and evasion of responsibility, undermine their confidence in their own abilities and foster contempt for women.

NOW will hold itself independent of any political party in order to mobilize the political power of all women and men intent on our goals. We will strive to ensure that no party, candidate, president, senator, governor, congressman, or any public official who betrays or ignores the principle of full equality between the sexes is elected or appointed to office.

We believe that women will do most to create a new image of women by *acting* now, and by speaking out in behalf of their own equality, freedom, and human dignity—not in pleas for special privilege, nor in enmity toward men, who are also victims of the current, half-equality between the sexes —but in active, self-respecting partnership with men.

Among the goals enunciated by NOW, are publicly supported child-care centers, abolition of state abortion laws, a reform in alimony laws to equalize responsibility, revision of tax laws to allow full deductions of all house-keeping and child-care expenses, and the reconstitution of housework into a professional career. As the only national organization in the movement, it is also the only one with organized lobbies to influence legislation on NOW issues.

In the recent New York mayoral election, NOW demonstrated outside the headquarters of all three mayoral candidates. NOW sent a series of questions to Procaccino, Lindsay, and Marchi as to their positions on NOW's seven-goal program. When the candidates failed to support or include the goals in their campaigns, NOW urged all women—according to NOW, 53% of New Yorkers—to withhold support from the men.

The seven goals were:

1. Prohibition of sex discrimination in education and job training.
2. Prohibition of sex discrimination in public accommodations and housing.
3. Tax deductions for child-care expenses of working parents.
4. Establishment of extensive child-care centers.
5. Establishment of vocational centers for homemakers.
6. Appointment of more women to city and party office.
7. Enforcement of prohibition of sex discrimination in employment.

The crowds on Fifth Avenue seemed amused by the sight of all the "ladies" (they were generally conventionally dressed) carrying such signs as "More sex in civil rights" and "Sex discrimination is as bad as race discrimination." NOW got considerable publicity for its demonstration.

NOW was founded in October, 1966, and by this act the renaissance of the women's movement in the United States was give a basis for growth. NOW was the matrix, but it presently exists outside the Women's Liberation Movement. The women's movement in America falls into three main categories: NOW, the Women's Liberation Movement, and the radical feminists. Amazingly enough, members of one of the most radical of the women's groups, the FEMINISTS, were once part of NOW, the archetypal reformist organization. In the fall of 1968, Ti-Grace Atkinson, then president of the New York chapter of NOW, together with a by-laws committee of eight people, proposed a rotary basis for the occupation of executive positions in the hope of distributing power more evenly. The motion of the by-laws committee was voted down; that same day President Atkinson tendered her resignation, issuing a statement at the same time.

It was the issue of equality within the women's movement that caused the break. Feminism had been reformulated in 1966 upon the realization that severe inequities existed in the opportunities, positions and options of men and women. The by-laws committee believed that the hierarchical structure of NOW, by placing power in the hands of a few, was translating to all the women below the executive level the very oppression that the movement was designed to counteract. In effect, the directors of NOW had become the "men" of the movement, acting as always to define, control and oppress those beneath them.

The by-laws committee felt that NOW's analysis of the inequities of the male-female relationship was too superficial. NOW wished only to obtain for women the same things that men had. Miss Atkinson and her supporters felt that that was merely continuing the cycle of oppression by concentrating power in the hands of the few.

Two days before the split in NOW, Betty Friedan, national president of the organization, had spoken at a

24

meeting to resolve the ideological conflict within the group. "I want to get women into positions of power," she said. To NOW, power and its manipulative use in society were apparently unobjectionable provided that women shared it. Ti-Grace Atkinson, at the same meeting, spoke the thoughts of many emerging radical feminists: "We want to destroy the positions of power . . . not to get into those positions."[4] And thus, the Divide.

The small groups of dissenters withdrew from NOW to form THE OCTOBER 17TH MOVEMENT. Eventually THE OCTOBER 17TH MOVEMENT became the FEMINISTS.

The FEMINISTS rank with NOW as the most highly organized of all women's groups. The group differed from NOW in their decision that the liberation of women must be based on a new political analysis. Herewith, a statement of their history from the FEMINISTS' own orientation packet:

On October 17th, 1968, in New York City, a group of feminists decided to begin a new kind of feminist movement: radical feminism. Most of us had been crossing organizational lines during the past year in the attempt to formulate an adequate solution to the persecution of women. But it had finally become evident that what we were groping for was not the sum of current ideas on women, but an approach altogether new, not only to feminism, but to political theory as well.

We decided to operate under the transitional name of the day of our beginning, October 17th, until we were prepared to outline our analysis of the class condition of women and its implications and to present our program for the elimination of that class condition. We are now ready to present our analysis and plan, and, therefore, announce the formation of our organization: the FEMINISTS.

June 13, 1969[5]

Before women are allowed to attend orientation meetings, they must first have read the packet, which the FEMINISTS mail out on request, and accept the principles outlined therein. The FEMINISTS is an organization with a rotating officership. More than executive duties are rotated. The work of the group is divided into two categories: routine and creative. Routine is typing, answering the telephone and envelope stuffing. Giving lectures, press conferences, writing position papers and giving radio and television interviews is creative work. Chairwomanship of the meetings is lot-determined and changes with every meeting. A secretary and treasurer, also chosen by lot, hold these offices for one month. No person takes a second turn at any task or office until everyone has had a turn at that work.

The allotment of work by drawing is the issue on which the FEMINISTS broke with NOW; it is integral to the philosophy and operation of the group. The belief that the permanent concentration of power in any segment of a group leads to the preponderant influence or authority of that segment and thus to the oppression of others is the basic tenet of their philosophy. Politically, the FEMINISTS are against oppression wherever it occurs. This is the ideological link among all radical feminist groups. Whether the realities of group interaction implement this belief will be discussed in a later chapter.

Experience has shown that an elite develops in political groups through the continual assignment of strategic skills to those already proficient at them. The lot system is an implementation of the belief that all people are equal. The gradated structure of prestige and power in societal groups is seen as a male organization of the abilities of groups and classes. It thus is marked as the basic inequity against which all radical egalitarians must struggle.

The FEMINISTS' literature proclaims as their goal

"the development of the multi-dimensional individual."
The lot method is seen as encouraging all members of
the groups. In the words of Jessica Furie: "It says that
some work is better than other work—but no person is
better than any other . . . It also says women—*all*
women—are capable of power—of leadership—but
that we no longer want the male values imposed on us
—that of hierarchy. It also says that—unless controlled
—women—in an anarchic situation—will grab control
—and dominate others—become "stars"—cater to the
press—and enter into a position they could not have
outside the movement—on top!'"

In the FEMINISTS, women with special abilities are
seen as "resource people." "When a member draws a
task beyond her experience, she may call on the
knowledge of other members but her own input and
development are of primary importance." All work
done for the group must be submitted to the group for
correction and approval. This practice of advise and
consent is expected to promote cooperation and inhibit
competition.

There is also shrewd political strategy in the "leaderless" system, perhaps an imitation of radical groups.
The FEMINISTS state it succinctly: "A group operating in this manner has a high survival factor . . . it will
not collapse because of its 'leaders' being picked off by
judicial arrests and can't be forced into unwanted
channels through a particularly strong member(s)
threatening to quit if the group doesn't wish to follow
her ideas."'

The FEMINISTS are a radical action group, their
actions being planned out of politics evolved from a
year's analysis of the oppression of women, its institutions, structures and instruments. In FEMINIST analysis, the education (socialization) of women determines
that theirs shall be dependent and underdeveloped in-
dividualities. It is a man's world: Men and men's institutions define womanhood and sanction femininity.

Women who fail to recognize and adopt the approved personality and behavior pattern will find themselves rebuked, scorned and pitied as failures.

If women are to accomplish their self-development, all institutions that prevent this realization must be eliminated. Men define women as childbearers. The maintenance of family life, with the wife-mother as all-loving, all-giving minister to the needs of husband and children, depends on women's identification of their desires and needs with the desires and needs of others.

The early FEMINISTS criticized sexual intercourse in its institutionalized forms, i.e., sexual intercourse as a drama of conquest and submission. One example is the venerable marriage manual that advises women: "Yield yourself with joyous abandon!" Modernity has increased male tyranny in the sex act. Before, it was the woman's duty to submit to the man; now it is her duty to have an orgasm, a real, vaginal orgasm, to show complete surrender to the man. It was Freud who invented the vaginal orgasm and described the clitoral orgasm as the failure of a woman to attain full femininity. This theory of the double orgasm is the archetype of the projection of male sexuality on the female and the full definition of woman as an incomplete man. The notion of the vaginal orgasm as a separate anatomic and biologic entity has been proven physiologically invalid. If a false biology of women can be invented to satisfy the dominant-submissive theory and be accepted for decades, it is clear that sexual intercourse is indeed an institution through which women have been taught, and men have learned, to expect from sex whatever pleases men even if it ignores the nature of women's fulfilment. As with all institutionalized activities, individual needs have been reformed and converted to fit formalized behavior.

It was not at first true that the FEMINISTS was a rigidly structured group. Increasingly, however, discipline and agreement with all group policies were required. Completion of assignments, attendance at both

28

meetings and actions were made compulsory. To quote from the orientation kit, which is the product of the doctrinaire caucus led by Ti-Grace Atkinson: "A single action which goes against the will of the group, constitutes an exploitation of the group, or seriously endangers its work or survival, is grounds for expulsion. Expulsion of a member requires a two-thirds majority decision of all members present at a meeting about which notification has been sent to all members at least ten days in advance . . .

"Any member missing more than one-quarter of the meetings in any given month forfeits voting privileges until the third consecutive meeting of that individual's renewed attendance. Should this occur three times in a three-month period without a valid excuse (e.g. employment or illness), the person involved is no longer a member of the FEMINISTS. She can reapply for membership if she wishes." (The application must be in writing.)

"We have a membership quota: that no more than one-third of our membership can be participants in either a formal (with legal contract) or informal (e.g., living with a man) instance of an institution of marriage."

The rules increased until every aspect of behavior at meetings was covered. The disciplinary tract of the group grew to resemble a penal code: The use of the term "penalizing" to describe the rules might be an ironic reference to Miss Atkinson's oppression of the group in the name of revolutionary discipline. To most of the group this came to seem little different from the male authoritarianism the FEMINISTS had formed to combat.

In the summer of 1969, when many members of the group were on vacation, the Atkinson caucus, headed by Miss Atkinson, Sheila Cronan, and Pamela Kearon, recast the analysis accomplished by the group in the past year, rewrote it, and produced several position papers and an orientation kit with which none of the vacationing members would have agreed.

The result was that the group broke up in the fall (1969) leaving five members in the FEMINISTS. This detailed account of the disintegration of the FEMINISTS (the first group) has been given because frequent alliances, ententes, coalitions and dissension are common to the three-year-old WL Movement although the causes of disintegration are as varied as the groups.

Since the autumn of 1969, the FEMINISTS have rigidified their politics and approach to society. It is not too much to say that the group as it is now constituted has made a politics of the neuroses of its members. In their analysis of love, the group has correctly identified the exploitive and destructive aspects of love as practiced in society but without recognizing the existence or possibility of emotionally satisfactory sexual relationships. "We must destroy love (by definition an institution)." Love is seen only as a tool of the powerful class, as an institution that socializes and instructs women into the dependency of the female role. "Love promotes vulnerability, dependence, possessiveness, susceptibility to pain, and prevents the full development of her human potential by directing all her energies outward in the interests of others. Love is a self-defense developed by the female to prevent her from seeing her powerless situation; it arises from fear when contact with reality provides no alternative to powerlessness."

These ideas evoke Eldridge Cleaver's analysis of the sexual and racial hierarchy wherein the most powerless people, black males and white females, are preoccupied with love: black males fantasizing themselves into great seducers, white females, living for love, both valuing themselves by the amount of admiration they can extract from others. This view of human relationships sees love as another counter in an age-old power struggle.

"We must destroy the institution of heterosexual sex which is a manifestation of the male-female role. Since

30

physical pleasure can be achieved in both sexes by auto-erotic acts," the FEMINISTS concluded that the act of sex is psychological in nature and that that psychology is dominance-passivity. Sexual relations as they now exist are structured to support male oppression of the female. Ti-Grace Atkinson suggests the possibility of non-exploitive physical relations (outside political contexts), which would "then be an extension of communication between individuals and would not necessarily involve genital emphasis."

Physical relations as they occur now in the context of exploitive and hostile male-female relations and, as a means of forcing child bearing on women, are therefore allusive of assault. Ti-Grace Atkinson equates marriage with the vaginal orgasm as a political construct of the male to justify the woman's role in sexual intercourse.

Thus the FEMINISTS' orientation kit contains the following questions in large, attention-grabbing type: "WOMEN DO YOU KNOW THE FACTS ABOUT MARRIAGE? DO YOU KNOW THAT RAPE IS LEGAL IN MARRIAGE? DO YOU KNOW THAT LOVE AND AFFECTION ARE NOT REQUIRED IN MARRIAGE? DO YOU KNOW THAT YOU ARE YOUR HUSBAND'S PRISONER?" The facts presented under these questions are indeed true. By law, you must have sexual intercourse to have a valid marriage, but this law also can be used to benefit women; they can sue for divorce if their husbands are impotent. It is also true that, in the majority of states, if a wife lives apart from her husband, he can sue for divorce.

It is the conclusion drawn from these facts that is startling. Marriage exists for, and is a condition of, rape, enslavement and imprisonment. It appears that rather than constituting a political organization to annihilate sex roles, the FEMINISTS is an organization to eradicate sexuality and the emotions. "A person is a

31

materiality." If we are such stuff as revolutions are willed by, we are also the creatures of our biology.

The use of such phrases as "the tyranny of complete subjectivism," when deprecating [and I use deprecate here in its original religious sense of a prayer that an evil be removed, for there is a self-righteous tone to recent FEMINIST literature) anything less than total commitment to the revolution (i.e., creation of "a space clear of male intrusion") suggests that Pamela Kearon's judgment is vitiated by her desire to reject biological nature and emotive existence.

I am saying that the philosophy and politics of the FEMINISTS, as they are now formulated, demonstrate by their repressive nature that they have been evolved out of the anxieties and fears of the members. By arguing against subjective actions in the group rather than combating the clear misogyny of men's magical concepts of women, the groups have shown themselves thoughtless, frantic and unresponsive to new stimuli and other voices. The FEMINISTS, writes Pamela Kearon, ask that people act before they feel, ask that they invest ends with more significance than means, to invent a wholly willed, wholly determined life as the means of achieving a new society. The FEMINISTS "cannot wait on the feelings of individual members, which are infinitely changeable."[8]

The signs and posters carried by NEW YORK RADICAL WOMEN in September, 1968, used strong language to compare the Miss America Pageant with the sale and prostitution of women. As Carol Hanisch wrote, our actions "hardly raised any woman's consciousness and really harmed the cause of sisterhood. Miss America and all beautiful women came off as our enemies instead of as our sisters who suffer with us . . . One of the reasons we came off anti-woman, besides the posters, was our lack of clarity. We didn't say clearly enough that we women are all *forced* to play the Miss America role—not by beautiful women but by men for whom

32

we have to act that role and by a system that has so well institutionalized male supremacy for its own ends."

The members of NYRW had come from disparate backgrounds. The influences of various political experiences and the philosophies assimilated from them were at work in the planning and implementation of the Miss America protest. For example, elements of Yippie language and psychology informed the protest. Miss Hanisch observed: "The Miss America protest was a zap action, as opposed to person-to-person group action. Zap actions are using our presence as a group and or the media to make women's oppression into social issues."⁹ Frequently since then feminists have formed the practice of not speaking to men and of only giving leaflets to women during the demonstrations. At the time of the Miss America protests, feminists were making uncritical use of the language and tactics of the New Left. The coronation of a sheep as Miss America is the direct analogue of the New Left's nomination of a pig for the presidency at the Democratic Convention in Chicago.

The Miss America protest evoked repressive measures and hostility ranged from taunting the picketing feminists and sending hate letters addressed to "Dear Ugly" to police surveillance of the meetings. The mayor of Atlantic City requested information about their plans, and Carol Giardina of Gainesville, Florida, women's liberation was fired for her participation in the demonstration. A member of NYRW was arrested and booked for throwing a stink bomb.

NYRW returned to New York with the idea of holding a fund-raising party to defray the cost of defending those women arrested during the Miss America protest. On Halloween the "politicos" in the group—a faction opposed to the "feminists"—conceived of holding a fund-raising event in a graveyard and charging the public for admission to guerrilla theatre, live music and mixed-media happenings. This event never materialized, but the intended locale suggests the "politicos' " enthusiasm for street theatre as political action. After the Women's Convention in Chicago in November, 1968, NYRW divided into three groups, designated Groups One, Two and Three. The groups were determined by lot. This division came about partially because of the unwieldy size of the group: Attendance was too large for consciousness-raising and also too large for unanimity as to the goals and purpose of the group. NYRW was also divided into smaller units because of personality conflicts (actually political) within the group.

While apparently structureless, the meetings had come to be dominated by a few women with particularly vivid personalities. It was hoped that dividing the group would separate these controlling women and break their hegemony. The political basis for this was the belief of many NYRW women that consciousness-raising should be a means to the development of a politics and not an end in itself. Women in the group also felt that consciousness-raising was particularly suited to the highly articulate women of the middle and upper classes and that these women were able to gain an ascendancy over the group through their proficiency in this central activity of the group.

Janine Sade's description of the pattern of events in Group Two is probably most accurate when applied to NYRW before the split. The dynamic feeling that she described is a recurrent one within the movement. "They (the groups) were small, so that every member could be heard, but the tendency was towards a takeover by those with the most insistent voices."

It is important to remember that the asserted philosophy of NYRW was the practice of democracy in the planning and implementation of all group activities, and a strict avoidance of the development of leaders and spokeswomen. Many radical groups have tried to practice this philosophy.

The division of NYRW into three groups proved a mistake. There was no system of communication

34

among the three groups so that women often didn't know when and where the inter-group meetings were held. The huge NYRW meetings had offered a diversity of opinions and lively discussions. Much of this was lost after the group divided. Division by lot separated women from their friends and sometimes from stimulating thinkers. Many of the 150 women who had been coming to NYRW were not yet ready to participate actively in smaller groups because they lacked knowledge of the feminist political tradition past and present.

Group One, later called REDSTOCKINGS, was perhaps the most cohesive of the groups. Group One led the New York women's action at President Nixon's inauguration. This feminist participation in the 1969 anti-inaugural demonstrations was the next event that shaped the Women's Liberation Movement in New York.

The 1969 anti-inaugural demonstrations were a coalition of many dissenting groups, dominated by the radical Left. The NYRW coalition went as a women's auxiliary, unconscious of what that would mean. The theme of the women's liberation action was the failure of the vote to effect changes in the quality of life of American women. The century of struggle that ended in the vote had not brought forth the deterioration of the inequities that burden women in every area, in every class, and in every aspect of their identities. NEW YORK RADICAL WOMEN were to burn their voter registration cards to dramatize this theme.

Ellen Willis, a member of NEW YORK RADICAL WOMEN at the time, gives an account of the humiliation and awakening the feminists suffered that January.

Mobe's ad in the *Guardian* calls for an end to the war and freedom for black and Spanish people. No mention of women's liberation. Women in another group want to ask men to destroy their voter cards. Apparently they have interpreted the action as a simple protest against electoral politics, rather

35

than a specifically feminist rejection of appeasement-by-ballot.

I get the funny feeling that we're being absorbed. Will we get the chance to deliver our message, or are we just there to show our support for the important (i.e. male-oriented) branches of the left? Our group decides to confront this issue with a speech attacking male chauvinism in the movement.

Dave Dellinger introduces the rally with a stirring denunciation of the war and racism.

'What about women, you schmuck,' I shout.

'And, uh, a special message from women's liberation,' he adds.

Our moment comes. M., from the Washington group, stands up to speak. This isn't the protest against movement men, which is the second on the agenda, just fairly innocuous radical rhetoric—except that it's a good-looking woman talking about women. The men go crazy. 'Take it off!' 'Take her off the stage and fuck her!' They yell and boo and guffaw at unwitting double entendres like 'We must take to the streets.' When S., (Shulamith Firestone) who is representing the New York group, comes to the mike and announces that women will no longer participate in any so-called revolution that does not include the abolition of male privilege, it sounds like a spontaneous outburst of rage (rather than like a deliberate statement of the politics of women's liberation).

By the time we get to the voter card business, I am shaking. If radical men can be so easily provoked into acting like rednecks (a women's liberation group at the University of North Carolina was urinated on by male hecklers at a demonstration) what can we expect from others? What have we gotten ourselves into?

Meanwhile Dellinger has been pleading with

us to get off the stage, 'for your own good.' Why isn't he telling them to shut up?

Just yesterday many of the women were arguing against Shulie's statement on the grounds that in spite of their chauvinism, movement men are basically our allies, and we shouldn't embarrass them in front of the straight press! As it turns out, none of the aboveground papers so much as mentions the women's action. Even the *Guardian* mysteriously neglects to report the second speech.

The whole fiasco has forced me to do some thinking. Without realizing it, I've held two contradictory views of women's liberation. On the one hand, I recognize the black analogy and need for separate groups free from male bias and male control. I know that the socialist revolutions have not eliminated male supremacy, that Soviet women still bear the burden of domestic responsibility, that machismo still flourishes in Cuba. But until now, I've also assumed that women's liberation was part of the radical movement, that one of our essential functions, in fact, was to bring masses of women into the left. (Note that at this point the contemporary feminists were not yet focused on the goal of self-determination for women.) Washington has destroyed that illusion. How can it be good for women to join a movement whose ideology, history and practice have been created by their oppressors? We need, not only separate groups, but a separate movement, free of preconceptions, which will build an analysis of women's oppression that is rooted in our day-to-day experience and base on that analysis our own revolutionary program. Radical men will stop oppressing us and make our fight their own when they can't get us to join them on any other terms.

Most of the women in New York's counterinaugural delegation have come to the same conclusions. We decide to form an action group based on a militantly independent, radical feminist consciousness.[10]

This group, formed by Shulamith Firestone and Ellen Willis, was the nascent REDSTOCKINGS. I shall make clear how the group developed away from this concept of militant activism and radical feminism.

According to Shulamith Firestone, REDSTOCKINGS was formed as a new action group when the women returning from the anti-inaugural demonstrations were unable to convince other NEW YORK RADICAL WOMEN of how badly they had been treated. Like WITCH, REDSTOCKINGS was formed as a radical group within the NYRW, not as a splinter group. The name REDSTOCKINGS was a play on blue stockings: the epithet for the women of an earlier era who encroached on the male world of learning and literary tastes and who were often ridiculed for their supposedly unnatural or affected interest in the male sphere. REDSTOCKINGS demands that women be freely given the right to operate in any sphere they choose. This is a centuries-old cry. Women must be free to invent their futures.

The action for which the early REDSTOCKINGS received the most publicity and which made the group known throughout the Women's Liberation Movement was the demonstrations at the New York legislature's 1969 abortion reform hearings. REDSTOCKINGS invaded the hearings for the abortion laws at a time when liberal legislators were trying to pass an abortion reform law. These legislators urged the women to cease disrupting the sessions and stated that they were only hurting their cause. Liberals everywhere, and women outside the feminist movement, agreed with this opinion.

REDSTOCKINGS broke up the sessions because laws that defined women's choices were being made by men. Once again, the lives of women were being bound and ruled by men. REDSTOCKINGS then held a con-

38

sciousness-raising session that was open to the public in which sisters testified about their personal experiences with abortion before an audience of both men and women. This was the beginning of REDSTOCKINGS' agitation to open the topic of abortion to public debate. It brought the group approval from feminists throughout the nation. They denounced Assemblyman Blumenthal's bill, which would have reformed the abortion law, as ineffectual, and wrong in the first place because it excluded the testimony of women from the lawmaking process which decided their fate.

Two constructs seem to underlie REDSTOCKINGS: sisterhood and consciousness-raising. Some members of REDSTOCKINGS developed the language and psychology of sisterhood, which is basic to modern feminism. This is not to say that the word sister or feminine solidarity is not practiced by other groups of women in other cities, but REDSTOCKINGS has the most strongly verbalized pro-woman line of all the groups.

This has involved rejecting the Marxist ideology that women will be liberated when capitalism is overthrown. REDSTOCKINGS believes that liberating women has priority above every other idea; it dispenses with formal political language and finds the key to a woman's liberation in her understanding of her experience. It bases political understanding on woman culture: "We regard our feelings as our most important source of political understanding . . . we see the key to our liberation in our collective wisdom and our collective strength." But this means opposing women's wisdom and concepts of self to the matrices that already exist—here all feminists must smile ironically at the use of the word matrix for the basis of male ideology and male-oriented reality. The following paragraphs come from REDSTOCKINGS' statement of principles:

"We take the woman's side in everything. We ask not if something is 'reformist,' 'radical,' 'revolutionary,' or 'moral.' We ask: is it good for women or bad for women?

We are critical of all past ideology, literature and philosophy, products as they are of male supremacist culture. We are re-examining even our words—language itself.

We take as our source the hitherto unrecognized culture of women, a culture which from long experience of oppression developed an intense appreciation of life, a sensitivity to unspoken thoughts and the complexity of simple things, a powerful knowledge of human needs and feelings.

This anti-intellectualism has proven to be the stumbling block of REDSTOCKINGS. In meetings members are unwilling, fearful and sometimes unable to move from an intuitive assessment of their experience to sociological understanding of what happened to them and why it has happened. Also REDSTOCKINGS has not made clear the distinction between the political idea of thought reformation through the shared experiences of small groups and the social stereotype of women as intuitive and specific creatures. The FEMINISTS make the shrewd criticism that the pro-woman line and consciousness-raising stop at a purely reflective and passive knowledge of the nature of women's oppression and then forgive women everything because they are oppressed.

Nevertheless REDSTOCKINGS has made some splendid statements about the condition of women. More than that, it has made progress in overcoming the inhibitions that many women, both inside and out of radical politics, feel about relating to an all-female group or in working for feminism, which is still often regarded as the preoccupation of maladjusted, dissatisfied, frustrated women. Irene Peslikis of REDSTOCKINGS identifies these defenses as:

Thinking that our man is the exception and therefore, we are the exception among women.

Thinking that individual solutions are possible, that we don't need solidarity and a revolution for our liberation.

Thinking that women's liberation is therapy. This, whether or not you belong to the organization, implies that you and others can find individual solutions to problems, for this is the function of therapy. Furthermore, the statement expresses anti-woman sentiment by implying that when women get together to study and analyze their own experience it means they are sick but when Chinese peasants or Guatemalan guerrillas get together and use the identical method, they are revolutionary.

Thinking that because we have an educational privilege and can talk in abstracts, we are somehow exempt from feeling oppression directly and talking about it honestly and, therefore, think of personal experience as something low on the ladder of values (class values).

Thinking that women consent to their own oppression . . . This is a statement which puts the blame on the oppressed group rather than on the oppressor class which ultimately uses brute force to keep the oppressed where they are. It is an anti-woman and anti-people statement.

Thinking that only institutions oppress women as opposed to other people. This implies that you have not identified your enemy, for institutions are only tools of the oppressor. When the oppressor is stopped, he can no longer maintain his tools and they are rendered useless. Present institutions and our feelings about them should be analyzed in order to understand what it is we want or don't want to use in the new society.

Thinking in terms of them and us. This implies that you are setting yourself off or apart from women (the people). In doing this, you neglect to recognize your own oppression and your common interest with other people as well as your stake in revolution.

Thinking that you can educate the people. This implies that you are educated, and you will get a revolution going by teaching other people what you know. Education does not bring on revolutions; but consciousness of our own oppression and struggle might. Unfortunately formal education and political consciousness do not usually coincide. *Even* (italics mine) formal education in Marxism-Leninism tends to make people think that they know more than they really know. When we think of what it is that politicizes people, it is not so much books or ideas but experience.

Thinking that male supremacy is only a psychological privilege with 'ego' benefits as opposed to a class privilege with sexual and economic benefits. The former implies considerable individual variation among men, therefore permitting you to find an individual solution to the problem.

It is possible to argue with the dismissal of male oppression as psychologically based—the theory that men need women to make them feel good—as an examination of the Stanton-Anthony Brigade's "politics of the ego" will show. Aside from this, the REDSTOCKINGS' analysis of free love is incisive and not to be denied; however, it is true that members of the group are living with men on a free-love basis, and there is a strong faction within the group that wants to focus group politics on constraining men to be faithful to these relationships and to treat women as equals within their marriages. This faction does not apply a radical analysis to the constructs of love and marriage but rather wants the group to help them find happiness within these institutions. The Peslikis paper continues:

Thinking that the relationships among men and women are already equal and thus immersing

42

yourself in utopian fantasies of free love in spite of the fact that the objective conditions deny it. Love between men and women, free or unfree, is millennial, not real, and if we want it, we will have to struggle for it.

Although REDSTOCKINGS was still a faction within NEW YORK RADICAL WOMEN at the time that this paper was written, the group as it now exists holds beliefs substantively the same as those that can be inferred from the statements presented above. While REDSTOCKINGS can be said to have failed in its announced attempt to cast out male ideologies (and, in fact, much of its writing and politics remains a reaction to the male world rather than an evolution of a female culture), it may be too early for any contemporary feminist group to have progressed beyond reaction to the old environment and institutions. Among the best things that REDSTOCKINGS produced is its condensation of the female reaction to the constant bombardment of male projections upon every woman. The group has produced magnificent verbalizations, which I feel to be so deeply, richly insightful that they change one's construction of reality, giving a new perception of the desperate competition for men and of the essential tragedy of sexual selection in Western society. For instance, here is the group's epiphanous definition of women's interests:

We define the best interests of women as the best interests of the poorest, most insulted, most despised, most abused woman on earth. Her lot, her suffering and abuse is the threat that men use against all of us to keep us in line. She is what all women fear being called, fear being treated as and yet what we all really are in the eyes of men. She is Everywoman: ugly, dumb (dumb broad, dumb cunt), bitch, nag, hag, whore, fucking and breeding machine, mother of us all. Until Everywoman is free, no woman will be free. When her beauty and knowledge is revealed and seen, the new day will be at hand.

This central idea of REDSTOCKINGS—that every woman has wisdom and knowledge through her own life experiences that will lead to working for revolutionary changes in her position—has become a commonplace of feminism. REDSTOCKINGS carries out this philosophical belief through the construct of leaderless meetings with a different chairwoman and secretary being chosen each time, although not by the lot system. The purpose of each meeting is for every sister to testify on the topic of the evening. After everyone in the group has testified, the group generalizes, from the various experiences related, to perceive how certain patterns of behavior, and occurrences formerly thought individual problems, are actually socially determined and can be politically contested.

The difficulty is that consciousness-raising often is dominated by the more verbal, articulate, better-educated and attractive personalities. Some women seem to use testifying to work out the problems of their private lives, without ever being able to extrapolate to an understanding and a political implementation of the group's experiences.

This happens despite the safeguard of a written guide for testimony, called *Protective Rules for Consciousness-Raising*. These rules are read by the group before each session. Basically they require each sister to bear testimony and, while doing so, to stick to specifics. Another strict rule is that the group hear every woman's particular testimony before moving on to generalization from the specific experiences. Judgment and comment on a sister's experiences are not allowed and, when a sister has a particular attitude to urge, she must state her reason for insisting on forcing the group or the person testifying to speak to her question.

After generalizations have been drawn and personal problems have been placed in a political context, the group then writes a position paper on its conclusions. As stated before, the tendency for some women to talk compulsively, often brilliantly, about their problems makes bearing testimony a very lengthy process. Also, the fact that some women have more compelling personalities and fascinating modes of recounting their experiences means that their feelings and ideas receive disproportionate emphasis when generalizations are finally made.

Furthermore, when the generalizations are written up, this is done on a volunteer basis, and women with the most experience tend to volunteer, gaining even more proficiency at this work. Gradually these people are looked to as undeclared leaders in the group, but this is a problem throughout the Women's Liberation Movement, in fact, in all groups.

REDSTOCKINGS' membership is almost entirely white, middle-class, educated. Single women outnumber married, and this has proven to be a problem as well when subject priorities for consciousness-raising are determined. Married women often feel attacked when sisters testify to a contempt for or wish to avoid marriage.

Increasingly since its inception, REDSTOCKINGS has concentrated on consciousness-raising and less on actions and demonstrations. The doctrine that all women can be politicized through increased awareness of their experiences, and group interpretation of them, has led to a preoccupation with this activity to the neglect of other areas. Activists think of REDSTOCKINGS as a purely personal collective.

REDSTOCKINGS does a lot of the initial work of introducing women, new to radical politics and women's liberation, to unfamiliar ideas by breaking down the pattern of seeing one's life in individual rather than socio-political terms. The group attracts large numbers of new recruits and does not turn anyone away. There is a formalized structure for bringing new people into the various REDSTOCKINGS groups. There is an orientation meeting once a month to accomplish this. The number of women attending REDSTOCKINGS has grown so rapidly that this formalization was necessary as well as was the division of the group into smaller units in which consciousness-raising was more practicable.

REDSTOCKINGS is somewhere on a line between women's liberation and radical feminism. NOW is a forerunner to, but has remained outside, the Women's Liberation Movement. The FEMINISTS, the NEW YORK RADICAL FEMINISTS and WITCH are radical feminists. Women's liberation is a phrase used for myriad political positions short of radical feminism: Its members are women who have joined the movement for social, economic and political equality for women but who do not envision revolutionary changes in society in order to gain these, nor the annihilation of sex roles or of marriage as an institution. Most of New York's more than one hundred feminist groups can be categorized under the heading of women's liberation.

WITCH (Women's International Terrorist Conspiracy from Hell), the group that evolved in the fall of 1968 from the "politicos" faction of NYRW, is a feminist organization for women already committed to radical change in our society. There are three covens in New York and covens in Washington, D.C., Chicago, and San Francisco, where the coven is said to be organizing hippie women, but none of them has any ties to the others. This is true also of the three covens within New York City.

Furthermore, the name WITCH and the picture it conjures up of dressing in costume and casting spells is frequently used by women's groups not affiliated with WITCH at all. For example, in Chicago SDS women wore witches' costumes to one demonstration without making it clear that they were not members of the Chicago coven. According to WOMEN: *A Journal of Liberation,* a collective of BREAD AND ROSES in Boston "dressed in black and masked, 'witched' Kenmore and Park Square dating bars on Halloween. They leafletted only women, giving them a women's liberation poem called *WITCH* and liberally plastered stores, banks and posters with women's liberation stickers. The response of women was so good they plan to return on regular trips Friday or Saturday nights."

WITCH has no party platform nor any central committee, consequently there is wide variation from coven to coven in the chosen foci for their activities and in their in-coven manner of relating to each other. There are three WITCH covens in New York, in different areas of the city, but each has developed along different lines; one of them has done more questioning and gone through more internal changes than the others. New York WITCH became a working entity as a result of the St. Valentine's Day action at the Bridal Fair in 1969.

At that time those women within NEW YORK RADICAL WOMEN who were later to be grouped as WITCHes alternated between guerrilla theatre actions and the development of a rigorous analysis of the institutions that oppress women. WITCH identified marriage as one of the capitalist bases of the oppression of women. The group decided to have a demonstration attacking the businessmen who profit from the institution of marriage and thereby to highlight this economic reinforcement of the oppression of women.

The Bridal Fair is a convention held to sell the appurtenances of marriage to the girls who attend it with their mothers. Sell an idea and the product will sell itself. The whole purpose of the booths, exhibits and fashion shows at the fair is to romanticize and embellish the marriage ceremony as the most important day in a woman's life: The purchase of a wedding gown is the creation of a memory and the wedding itself an elevation into the ecstasy and acceptability of wifehood. They sell and sell and sell, and the mothers and daughters buy eagerly, focused as they are on proving how much they are worth on the marriage market. The conspicuous expense and luxurious panoply of the ceremony prove the bride's desirability for all time. She is among the chosen.

This early WITCH action was unsuccessful. It was poorly organized, but the real difficulty was that the group was trying to communicate a sophisticated idea to apolitical women gathered in pursuit of a stabilizing identity: wifehood. A couple of the feminists wore witch costumes; they leafletted the women, and they performed a skit, but it was cold outdoors and the skit called for more props than the fledgling organization had time to get together. The brides-to-be and their mothers experienced the entire encounter as an attack on them, as could have been expected. They felt that they were being ridiculed for not being more than housewives and mothers.

The simultaneous demonstration at the Valentine's Day Bridal Fair in San Francisco had a less austere approach to the women attending the fair. Pamela Allen, who had been a founding member of NEW YORK RADICAL WOMEN, was involved in the California demonstration. Their leaflet was different in tone: more California-gentle and non-directive. It was meant to be persuasive rather than logically compelling, leaving the women to come and find out for themselves. It said that, as women, we have all been subjected to the same pressures and conventions; if you're interested in talking about this, come and see us. Some women did.

The NEW YORK RADICAL WOMEN who had stayed away from the Bridal Fair demonstration were estranged further by its failure, and for a time there was a pause in communications between WITCH and the other NEW YORK RADICAL WOMEN. WITCH went on growing in size and eventually divided into three covens. For the first year of its independence New York WITCH has alternated between actions and consciousness-raising, but of a less structured kind than that practiced by REDSTOCKINGS. Yet women in WITCH are perhaps more analytical of their experiences and politically sophisticated, although neither group has formalized a political doctrine at the end of its first year.

In speaking of WITCHes, it is necessary to explain that many radical women, both in and out of feminism, don't want to deal with the media or publicize the internal workings of their organizations. Their reasoning has a sound basis: Publicity is the American way of neutralizing originality and radicalism by assimilation. A new orientation of ideas and concentration of energy used to have several decades to enrich, fuse and analyze itself before publicizing its existence. Women's liberation is being seized upon by the media as an idea whose time has come. Vulnerability to publicity and the hunger for fame has killed many ideas and even more people. Haight-Ashbury died in two summers. To some radical women, a detailed journalistic description of the movement can only weaken it. They would prefer examination of feminism to come from within the movement and its circulation to be restricted to movement women.

At the same time, my feeling is that it is more important to get down the myriad significant happenings of what will surely be one of the great revolutions in the history of Western civilization. To do this without providing material for the Justice Department—of the kind that *The New York Times* has revealed is, by a "long-standing policy," habitually shown to the government upon demand—is difficult and absolutely necessary for any responsible social commentator. WITCHes and many other radical women will not be identified or described in detail.

While two New York covens have remained more like the original WITCH coven, one has gone through considerable self-examination, developing along the line of a more empathic relationship with all women. This coven can be said to have a more pro-woman line. Members of this particular coven have developed a communal support of each other, visit each other constantly, call special meetings when a sister has a problem and are committed to an intense examination of, and struggle against, the oppression of women.

All the identifiable feminist groups receive constant requests from women for information on joining groups or on forming groups of their own. These requests come from high schools and universities in the metropolitan area. WITCHes in addition attend benefits, rallies and demonstrations in support of women unionists, welfare-rights groups and any group of women questioning their position in society or seeking a radical perception of their roles.

Ivy Bottini, president of New York NOW, was a chief organizer of the Congress to Unite Women, which was attended by New York feminists and women from other cities in the Northeast on the weekend before Thanksgiving, 1969, the weekend of the Panther demonstration in New Haven. In this mobile age, feminists often travel to Boston, Ithaca, Washington, D.C., or Chicago for demonstrations or assemblies. The Congress was called "to unify women's organizations to work toward goals that affect all women's lives."

The Congress was closed to men and to the media. Bill Baird, the head of a birth control movement on Long Island, and some followers of indeterminate sex, demonstrated against being barred from the Congress. A major television network was allowed in with the provision that it would not film the actual events or the participants of the Congress (many women felt their jobs would be endangered if their feminist sympathies were known). The network crew violated their agreement at once by filming people at the Congress who had not agreed to be interviewed. They also filmed a Boston women's liberation happening: The group had their hair cut to demonstrate their refusal to conform to the socializing and controlling standards of feminine dress. Angered by this, members of the Planning Commission disappeared with the film. It was said to have been burned.

Friday, November 21, the first night of the Congress, a slide presentation on women's image throughout history was shown and a discussion of women's situation today followed. The program on Saturday was divided into three parts. Workshops on women's questions were held in the morning and in the afternoon, and the New Feminist Repertory Theatre performed in the evening.

The topics of the twelve workshops were: 1) Early Childhood: Care and Education; 2) Education (with stress on secondary and college levels); 3) Employment—Do equal employment opportunities exist for women?; 4) Family structure—the institution of marriage as instrumental to the maintenance of male supremacy; 5) The "Feminine Image"—its dehumanizing aspects; 6) How Women are Divided: class, racial, sexual and religious differences; 7) Love and Sex; 8) The Nature and Function of a Feminist Group; 9) Political Power—discussion of means of achieving the goals of the Women's Liberation Movement; 10) Reproduction and its Control; 11) The Sex-Role System; and 12) Women and the Law.

Women were free to attend the workshops of their interest. At the end of the discussion period, each workshop, morning and afternoon, redacted a resolution stating the group's thinking on the topic.

Sunday was devoted to a plenary session of all the workshops to discuss and decide which resolutions would be adopted by the Congress as a whole.

While discussions in the workshops often seemed confined to familiar ground, on Sunday an influx of radical women (to be distinguished from women radicals) and a growing ease with each other allowed the approximately 200 women attending the Congress to have some lively discussions. Women from several diverse organizations had participated in the planning of the Congress: City College Women's Liberation, Columbia Women's Liberation, DAUGHTERS OF BILITIS, THE FEMINISTS, MEDIA WOMEN, NOW, NEW YORKERS FOR ABORTION LAW REPEAL, REDSTOCKINGS, STUDENT HOMOPHILE LEAGUE, WITCH, WOMEN'S ACTION COMMITTEE of the World Fellowship, WOMEN'S CAUCUS of the Young Socialist Alliance, NEW YORK RADICAL FEMINISTS and WOMEN'S LIBERATION NO. 55. Women attending the Congress represented many more groups than those enumerated above. Some women came from out of town. As a group, the Congress was young, friendly, comfortably dressed (few wore high heels or girdles), numbered some mothers with their babies among its population, and was intent on women's questions.

Women voted to create a permanent women's coalition for the Northeastern United States that would hold organizational meetings soon after the Congress.

Another group important to the development of New York's Women's Liberation Movement was the Thursday night "citywide" women's liberation coalition that held its meetings at the Washington Square "Peace" Church. This coalition was disbanded in December as a result of dissension on the New Haven Black Panther Demonstration that was held the same weekend as the Congress. The purpose of the coalition was to allow a women's liberation group whose size had become unmanageable to meet and support each other on actions while its members met elsewhere in small groups for radical projects and consciousness-raising. The politics of this "citywide" coalition were radical, or rather its member groups tended to be women radicals rather than radical feminists. The coalition meetings in the end were little more than a bulletin board. The women attending were not delegated representatives of their groups and consequently could not commit the group to any action. The result was that the proposals adopted by the coalition had little effect on its individual collectives.

At a typical meeting, young women, usually under 25, rose and recited their collective's progress, usually minimal, for instance, in organizing the secretaries at ITT or the attendants in a mid-town hospital. Women announced upcoming actions, shouted out their names and telephone numbers and asked interested women to contact them.

The Thursday night coalition supported most elements of the New Left: The Rainbow Coalition (The Black Panther Party, The Young Lords and The Patriots—radical whites from Appalachia), and Weatherman RYM'S I and II of SDS. Radical feminists criticized the coalition for expending its energies on so many non-feminist issues. Coalition members in turn made it clear that groups that concentrated on consciousness-raising, such as REDSTOCKINGS, were non grata at the coalition meetings.

On November 21st, Thursday Coalitionists, WITCHes, and other New York women were in New Haven demonstrating against the harsh conditions under which three pregnant Black Panther women were imprisoned. Many radical women demonstrated because the Panthers are culture heroes and are felt to be the victims of systematic oppression by the Justice Department.

Word had come down from New Haven that the lights in the pregnant women's cells were kept shining twenty-four hours a day; that their diet was inadequate for their pregnancies (Rose Smith gained only one pound from the second to the eighth month of her pregnancy); that they would have to labor and give birth under armed guard; and finally, that the government would take their babies from them and place them with the state.

New York women of radical persuasion decided to help stage a protest. Nanette Rainone announced the demonstration over "Womankind," a weekly feminist radio program. Dissension rose among the organizers on two issues: Were the prison conditions of the Panther women a women's issue and should REDSTOCKINGS and other non-action-oriented groups be invited to join? The decision they made was that any persecution or humiliation of women became a women's issue, and that all New York WL groups should be invited to join.

When the organizers returned to their groups, discussion continued. Some women feared that the Black Panthers, infamous for their arrogance, would co-opt the demonstration and transform it into a pro-Panther rather than a pro-woman demonstration. Finally the decision was made that women who wished to attend should go on an individual basis.

The women who did go to the demonstration had mixed reactions. A militant rally was held in front of the courthouse. The chants "Fuck Harvard! Fuck Yale! Get those Panthers out of jail!" (It was the weekend of the Harvard-Yale game) was standard leftist. Another chant was distinctly feminist: "Out of the house, Out of the ghetto, Out from under, Women unite!" This mixed rhetoric was the result of the analysis of the women radicals: "1)Women are committed to the struggle to radically change America in solidarity with our brothers, black and white; 2)Women are committed to playing a leadership role in this struggle; 3)Women are committed to raising issues which are particularly relevant to women in the struggle." Apparently women radicals are willing to support feminism, too.

The Black Panthers themselves are intolerant of the feminist analysis of women's oppression. The party thinks its own construction applies equally to men and women and to all oppressed peoples. Throughout the movement there seems to be a development away from the large publicity-gathering demonstration, that is by definition media-manipulated, and toward personal encounters with women outside the movement and pragmatic action to alleviate the injustices of women.

The Panther demonstration caused the final split in the "citywide" coalition. Some women who had participated in the protest felt that women's rights issues had been obscured and that it had turned into a demonstration in support of the Panthers. Their conclusion was that interested women should have gone as radical supporters and not as feminist representatives. Other women in the coalition took this to be a development away from support of militant groups and were vehement in their affirmations of the necessity of supporting the Movement (here they mean the New Left movement).

The reverberations of the break between the women disillusioned about alliances with the New Left, and the neo-Marxist women who were incapable of changing their primary commitment, continued to shake the organization. In December the Thursday night Coalition ceased to meet. It had been New York's nearest approach to a central headquarters for the women's movement. Now interested women from many groups are meeting to set up a WL Center with a library, telephone message service and a mimeograph machine.

The reactions of NEW HAVEN WOMEN'S LIBERATION are particularly interesting as they appear to indicate a trend of development of WL groups. Their reaction was primarily negative. They felt that they "learned much about the problems of working with movement groups who do not respect the individual or the goals of women's liberation. We learned about the serious division among the groups within the women's movement. The experience forced us to begin a serious examination of the relationships between the women's movement and other movements of the left; we began to question the value of mass demonstrations as a means to communicate with other New Haven women about women's liberation."[11]

Reaching out to women not already in the movement is the principal concern of New Haven WL. Since the summer of 1969, the organization implemented an ambitious plan of starting small groups for discussing women's rights in many areas and occupations. Liberation groups have been started on the feminists' jobs; at Yale, where an alliance was formed with the campaign to unionize female technical and clerical employees; in the feminists' own neighborhoods. Groups have also started in high schools, community schools and Yale graduate school. A newsletter, *Yale-Break,* serves as a communications link for all these activities.

The Panther demonstration had the effect of concentrating New Haven WL on feminist issues and on talking with other women.

A coalition of the high school women's liberation groups in New York was also formed in the late fall of 1969. The coalition holds general meetings so that the different high school groups may organize around agreed-on issues and share the experiences and problems of high school women in the metropolitan area.

Most of their demands would center on the curricula in their schools. The role of women in history is neglected in high school education, the early feminist movement and the sociology of sex roles not even discussed. The high school coalition is demanding woman studies to inform all students about women's heritage and to demonstrate that the role of women is a socially learned behavior phenomenon.

They are also demanding that all courses be made co-educational, and that the teaching of crafts and skills not be segregated according to sex. Their most radical demand is the dissemination of birth control information and contraceptives by their schools. Yet this demand is not as extreme as it would have seemed five years ago. In February, 1970, the school board in New York made public the rule that all high schools must have facilities for childbirth. This unprecedented facing of the fact of teen-aged pregnancies augurs a sympathetic ear for the demands of high school women.

The NEW YORK RADICAL FEMINISTS (NYRF) is the name for the aggregation of radical feminists founded by the Stanton-Anthony Brigade on December 5, 1969. The Stanton-Anthony Brigade, which was founded by women from the FEMINISTS and REDSTOCKINGS, Diane Crowthers, Shulamith Firestone, Ann Koedt, and Cellestine Ware, was begun in an effort to fill the political and organizational needs that had been

56

largely unmet by the feminist groups already in existence.

The origin of the founding cell's name tells much about the group's gestalt. The hyphenated name of the group is composed of the surnames of two of the outstanding leaders of the first generation of feminists: Elizabeth Cady Stanton, perhaps the boldest thinker of the movement, and Susan B. Anthony, the foremost agitator in the nineteenth century for women's right to vote. The Stanton-Anthony Brigade believes in the use of the "Sister System." This is the practice of members of the group working together in units of two or three chosen sisters on the projects at hand.

The NYRF has highly evolved, definite ideas of what its structure and ideology should be, the direction in which the member brigades should go, and how they should do this. All of these things have been indicated in its Organizing Principles, from which I quote.

"Nuclear leaderless/structureless groups of no more than 15, together with some minimal coordination among them, have already, in the short history of contemporary feminism, proved to be the organizational method best suited to our needs and goals. The dynamics of the small group, where women, over a period of time, develop a personal intimacy, a common political awareness arrived at together, and a group experience, in short, where women seal up the gaps among them to arrive at about the same place, foster—indeed, in our time, seem to be the preconditions—for a working internal democracy. Further we have found that within this cadre, women function best in units of two, occasionally three, of their own personal choice. Such a *Sister System* was common to the old feminist movement, and was a valuable aid in overcoming, by means of close mutual reinforcement and intersupplementation, the weakness and lack of confidence we have each acquired in different areas due to the constant battering from without. (Without here refers to the pressures of achieving self-realization in a man's world.)"

NEW YORK RADICAL FEMINISTS will only accept as fully active members those women who agree with the essentials of their political platform. Here are some quotes from their Manifesto:

"Radical feminism recognizes the oppression of women as a fundamental political oppression wherein women are categorized as an inferior class based upon their sex. It is the aim of radical feminism to organize politically to destroy this sex class system.

"As radical feminists we recognize that we are engaged in a power struggle with men, and that the agent of our oppression is man insofar as he identifies with and carries out the supremacy privileges of the male role. For while we realize that the liberation of women will ultimately mean the liberation of men from the destructive role as oppressor, we have no illusion that men will welcome this liberation without a struggle.

"Radical feminism is political because it recognizes that a group of individuals (men) have set up institutions throughout society to maintain this power.

"Politics of the Ego"

". . .We believe that the purpose of male chauvinism is primarily to obtain psychological ego satisfaction, and that only secondarily does this manifest itself in economic relationships." (This is the idea current among radical feminists of all groups that racism and sexism predated the formation of socio-economic systems.) "For this reason we do not believe that capitalism, or any other economic system, is the cause of female oppression, nor do we believe that female oppression will disappear as a result of a purely economic revolution. The political oppression of women has its own class dynamic. And that dynamic must be understood in terms previously called 'non-political'—namely the politics of the ego. (We're using the traditional rather than the Freudian, that is, the sense of individual self as distinct from others.)

". . . the male ego identity (is) sustained through its ability to have power over the female ego. Man establishes his 'manhood' in direct proportion to his ability to have his ego override hers, and derives his strength and self-esteem through this process. This male need, though destructive, is in that sense, impersonal. It is not out of a desire to hurt the woman that he dominates her and destroys her; it is out of a need for a sense of power that he necessarily must destroy her ego and make it subservient to his. Hostility to women is a secondary effect; to the degree that he is not fulfilling his own assumptions of male power, he hates women for not complying.

"As women we are living in a male power structure, and our roles become necessarily a function of men. The services we supply are services to the male ego. We are rewarded according to how well we perform these services. Our skill— our profession—is our ability to be feminine— that is, dainty, sweet, passive, helpless, ever-giving, and sexy. In other words everything to help reassure a man that he is primary.

". . . If we do not choose to perform these ego services, but instead assert ourselves as primary to ourselves, we are denied the necessary access to alternatives wherein we can manifest our self-assertion. Decision-making positions in the different job fields are closed to us; politics (left, right or liberal) are barred in other than auxiliary roles; our creative efforts are *a priori* judged not serious because we are females; our day-to-day lives are judged failures because we have not become 'real women.'

The itemization above of women's oppression would be agreed with by NOW and by most women in the Women's Liberation Movement. Radical feminism differs from either of these in not demanding that which men already have but in working for the eradication of domination and elitism in all human relationships. This would make self-determination the ultimate good and require the downfall of society as we know it today. The NYRF Manifesto continues:

"The oppression of women is manifested in particular institutions, constructed and maintained to keep women in their place. Among these are the institutions of marriage, motherhood, love, and sexual intercourse (the family unit is incorporated in the above). Through these institutions, the woman is taught to confuse her biological sexual differences with her total human potential. Biology is destiny, she is told." (Compare Dr. Spock) . . . "In each case *her* sexual difference is rationalized to trap her within it, while the male sexual difference is rationalized to imply an access to all areas of human activity.

"Love, in the context of an oppressive male-female relationship, becomes an emotional cement to justify the dominant-submissive relationship . . . Love, magical and systematically unanalyzed, becomes the emotional rationale for the submission of one ego to another. And it is deemed every woman's natural function to love.

"Radical feminism believes that the popularized version of love has thus been used politically to cloud and justify an oppressive relationship between men and women, and that in reality, there can be no genuine love until the need to *control* the growth of another is substituted by the love *for* the growth of the other.

"For the sake of our own liberation . . . we must begin to destroy the notion that we are indeed only servants to the male ego, and must begin to reverse the systematic crushing of women's egos by constructing alternate selves that are healthy, independent and self-assertive. We must, in short, help each other to transfer the ultimate power of judgment about the value of our lives from men to ourselves."

The NYRF does not see this Manifesto as the group's ultimate statement about the male-female role system, but rather views this Manifesto as an initial statement, part of a work in progress. The last sentence of the Manifesto concludes: "It remains for us as women to fully develop a new dialectic of sex class—an analysis of the way in which sexual identity and institutions reinforce one another."

In the first month of its existence the attendance at Stanton-Anthony Brigade meetings increased from five to forty women. The women who came to the meetings had varying degrees of commitment to radical feminism, knowledge of feminist history, and familiarity with the contemporary feminist movement. The group's attempt to plan its first action—a protest against male-female role differentiation as taught by Christmas toys —was abortive because of the conflict and lack of organization within the group.

At that point, it was decided by the original cell to de-centralize the organization into core groups, each of which is to take a six-month formative period in which it will follow the structural procedure set down in the Organizing Principles of the NYRF. Within the formative period, each group can increase its membership up to 15: preferably based on geographical location. There are also to be groups organized around the NYU Law School, the Feminist Repertory Ensemble (a group of actors and actresses staging feminist ideas), and possibly various professions.

NYRF has a three-stage orientation program as the required preliminary before membership as a full Brigade. In Stage I the core group is called a phalanx. Its members are to engage in a minimum of three months of consciousness-raising to increase awareness of the many insidious forms that the oppression of women takes and to build group solidarity.

The phalanx is expected to spend its last three months in reading and discussing literature of the current women's movement and feminist history and theory (preferably from direct sources). The purpose of this three-month period of reading and discussion is:

1) to acquaint each person with the broad spectrum of politics already apparent in the Women's Liberation Movement.

2) to discuss the position of radical feminism within this spectrum and to compare it with other views.

3) to acquaint each member of the group with her own history and to give her a sense of continuity within the feminist political tradition.

4) to give the group a good foundation in basic theory on which to build its own later analysis.

5) to give the group some basis on which to choose its name.

When a phalanx becomes a full Brigade its members must choose their name from the ranks of radical feminists; the Organizing Principles suggest the name of a feminist whose philosophy is in character with the aims of the group. The first group project will be to produce a booklet on the feminist whose name the group is adopting. "The total number of these booklets will form a cheap, easy to distribute, radical feminist library researched by movement women—a first step in erasing the bias and feminine fear of feminism created by the Fifty Year Ridicule."

Upon completion of the sixth-month study period, and when each individual member has signed the NYRF Manifesto, the group is expected to elect their first delegates to the NYRF Coordinating Body. These delegates will be rotated so that each member of the Brigade has served this office. It is also strongly suggested that the new Brigade "initiate an action from start to finish in which all the other Brigades—and perhaps selected outside groups—will be invited to participate. This includes doing all planning, preparatory work . . . press releases, invitations, etc., required for successful completion of the action."

Afterwards, the Brigade is regarded as an independent unit within NYRF, evolving its own course of winning women's liberation in whatever aspect and by whatever method it shall decide, including effective (as opposed to self-indulgent) action, serious analysis, work with the media, writing and publishing, films, lectures, etc.

The NYRF stipulates "We will work only with women reporters but will inform and penalize in an appropriate manner any reporter and medium that, for whatever reason, in tone or substance, presents distorted or partial information about our group. We will also seek to form a strong coalition with other women's rights groups in order to deal more effectively with the problems and potential of the media."

This rule of feminists of only talking to women in the media, and moreover, to those women whose previous work indicates that they will not distort reported material, is taken over from the black militant movement and is being increasingly and systematically applied throughout the movement.

The New York Media Project is an organization of men and women employed in the media institutions who are concerned to redirect the media from MASSCOMM to conscientious coverage of the critical social and political issues of today. In a process by now familiar, the women within the Project began to feel that their voices were not being heard, that their problems were not being fought and that they were treated as secondary to the important business of the organization. The women formed a caucus within NYMP and in September of 1969 this caucus became an autonomous organization of women working in the media institutions and interested in women's rights.

In mid-October, two members of the group were involved in a protest on their jobs that is exemplary of the concerns of the group. Lindsy Van Gelder and Bryna Taubman, reporters for the New York *Post* invoked a contract clause, allowing reporters to withhold their bylines when they wish. The two women informed the editors that they did not want by-lines on stories about women "whose only claim to fame was that they were wives of famous men."

Lindsy Van Gelder was assigned to write a profile of Mrs. Gil Hodges. In the words of *The New York Times* article on the case: "Mrs. Van Gelder accepted the assignment but asked that the story not carry her name since she objected to articles about women whose claim to newsworthiness was their marriage to famous men. The assignment was then given to someone else. Miss Taubman then joined Mrs. Van Gelder in her stand. They met with the executive editor (according to Bryna Taubman's account), who "spent two days wishing it was the Thirties so that he could fire us, and finally decided that it was. After long chats with him, in which he alternately threatened and cajoled us, we were fired for gross insubordination." At this point all guild members on the *Post* aligned themselves, though unwillingly, with the women as the firing was a violation of the rights guaranteed by guild contract. The guild demanded a grievance hearing with management, and the two reporters were reinstated. According to *The New York Times*: "Despite the reinstatement of the reporters . . . most of the *Post's* reporters have asked that their by-lines be kept off their articles until further notice."

The postscript to that incident is that a group of male reporters at the *Post,* as a "joke," dropped a note in Lindsy Van Gelder's mailbox announcing the formation of a men's rights group to be called PENIS (Prevent emasculation of our needs by the inferior sex).

MEDIA WOMEN puts out a newsletter with the double-edged title of *Women's Monthly*. It focuses on announcements of events in the WL Movement and offers debates on the varying positions within the movement. In the Statement of Purpose, the group "hopes to be a forum for the many voices of the movement. We address not only women who are committed, but also those who are just becoming aware or interested in women's rights. We view the newsletter as an instrument to draw more women into the movement by providing a guide to women's groups announcing actions, conferences, meetings . . . being a platform for sophisticated political discussion debate on the movement."

The capital of the art world is New York, and the discontent that became epidemic in America in the 60's manifested itself among artists in the determination to make it possible for an artist to earn a living from his work. The Art Workers' Coalition organized itself to effect change in the gallery-museum pantheon, and it has met with some success. WAR (Women Artists for Revolution) is the women's caucus of A.W.C., which was formed to insure that the interests of women artists should not be ignored in the reforms that were being made.

Among A.W.C.'s goals are "only one pay day" each week, instead of only one free day, at all museums in the country. (The A.W.C. was the most insistent of the groups that succeeded in the institution of free admission at the Museum of Modern Art on Mondays.)

Their goals are "to bring about fair representation of black and Puerto Rican artists in the museums of this city and to give black and Puerto Rican artists the encouragement which the present museum-gallery system has failed to give."

Near the bottom of the list comes "to bring about fair treatment of women artists and of artists without galleries." When the black and Puerto Rican artists negotiated with the museums, they were given a sympathetic ear and a substantial number of their demands were met. The women found that the A.W.C. was not supporting them in struggling for equal gains for women even though research revealed that women were even more underrepresented and discriminated against than blacks. This led to the formation of WAR, the women's caucus.

WAR aims "to make all women artists aware of the problems within themselves—their conditioning against success; to make the art world aware of the problems and discrimination faced by women artists; to demand a non-juried show of women's art at the Museum of Modern Art." WAR refuses even a jury composed of women on the grounds that most women experts in the art world are conditioned to discriminate against women.

Boston's women's liberation groups constitute the other large East Coast movement and they are socialist oriented. BREAD AND ROSES is the parent organization within which approximately 200 women are organized into collectives to work on projects. Some of the proj-

66

ects are: Abortion Repeal; Day-Care Centers; Women's Classes on Marxism; Karate; Organizing Secretaries and Clinic Workers; Play group for children; Supporting GE Strikers; Married Couples' Discussion Group; and Research on History of American Women. The organization holds weekly orientation meetings for new members and publishes a newsletter. BREAD AND ROSES seems to feel a political sympathy with New York WITCH, or at least with one of the covens. Their membership is mostly women who have had a long-term commitment to radical politics. This distinctive background has limited the development of the Boston women at the same time it has furnished them with organizing skills.

BREAD AND ROSES is so strongly influenced by Weatherman that its women sometimes accept SDS political positions that admittedly don't "stem from their own understanding or experience." Other times B&R women consciously rebel, but the form of their rejection is dictated by the positions that Weatherman already occupies. B&R dissent tends to be cautious. Their characteristic attitude is that they would never want to go against SDS or the Panthers. "Weatherman is important because they see the same problems we do, but our reactions and partial answers are different . . . The problem that many of us face," wrote members of one B&R collective, "is that our women's movement has not yet developed a sense or complete strategy of what is 'right.' "

This B&R analysis shows that socialism is still felt to be their main objective, and that B&R women feel it necessary to justify themselves whenever socialism causes do not take top priority. It is surprising to find politically knowledgeable women apparently ignorant of the lessons supplied by the early feminist movement in America. It is surprising to find women still feeling guilty for working in their own interest and concentrating on freeing themselves. Understanding has come to modern feminists that a woman cannot become a trustworthy radical until she enters politics on the basis of an understanding of her own oppression qua woman.

Implicit in the B&R uneasiness at being at odds with Weatherman and other New Left groups is the belief that WL is not a legitimate political concern. The priorities established in their analysis are worthy of comment as they are typical of the Marxist position within feminism:

> Radicals must confront the possibility that successful third world attacks against American imperials will create an economic and political crisis in this country that could swing toward either fascism or a communist revolution.
>
> Because so many Americans benefit from imperialism, in the short run, any threat to that system could intensify the backlash and create a government based on racism and anti-communism. We must show these people that they have a political stake in giving up these short-range benefits for the obvious long-range benefits of a society free of economic exploitation, male chauvinism, and racial oppression.
>
> In fact, more and more people in this country —women, farm and factory workers, GI's—are realizing that they don't have any *real* power in relation to the class that runs and profits from this country. Our problem is to reach people and organize them with political tools so that they have gut understanding of why that exploitation and powerlessness must end.

The analysis above seems more representative of the thinking of radicals than that of radical women, but it is the thinking of a very large faction within feminism. This analysis does not concentrate on women and on their realization of autonomy. In fact, women's concerns seem to be just one of the issues to them, and not necessarily the first on their list.

B&R only enters the truly feminist continuum when it states that women of all classes are equally oppressed and that racism will be ended by women working together to end their exploitation as women. Still, as always, the position papers begin with the socialist idea of the mystique of the people and work from this to the discussion of women. When a B&R collective does come to strongly feminist conclusions, it then will state that the mobilization of women in their "individual" interest is justified by the strong role that women will then be able to play in overthrowing the ruling class. The collective does not distinguish all men as the ruling class even though their feminist analysis leads to that conclusion.

An example of this is the inclusion in the same position paper of two such definitively different viewpoints as the following: 1) "This condition of oppression is quantitatively—not qualitatively—worse for women married to men working in factories than it is for women married to white-collar professionals" and 2) "The time women will be able to fight and defeat such racism will be when they are moving collectively and fighting to end their real exploitation and oppression as women." In other words, feminism is but a means to ending racism. "Such a model for individual change grows out of our feeling that a socialist revolution means that we—as women—are going to be part of the class that will overthrow the ruling class from power and share in the task of serving the real needs of the people." Their belief that women are united with poor and black men as oppressed people is irreconcilable with their earlier assertion that the wives of both factory and white-collar workers are oppressed by the woman's role within the nuclear family. It is irreconcilable with the fact that women as a group have different interests from men.

It is not until the final third of this position paper that B&R focuses on the problems that women have in working with radicals of the New Left.

Finally, as women, we are very angry at Weatherman's male chauvinism in theory and action . . . The machismo and militarism characterizing Weatherman action and literature do not merely reflect tactical errors of improper application of theory. Indeed, their male chauvinism stems from a basic misunderstanding of the nature of women's oppression.

They believe that women are oppressed by male chauvinism but are also racist oppressors in an imperialist society. They admit that the nuclear family is oppressive, an oppression that crosses class lines, but state that many women also have 'white-skin privileges.' Their logic is that the primary contradiction is imperialism. Strategically they conclude that the priority is to fight imperialism, to engage women in anti-imperialist struggles, to support blacks, and to fight male chauvinism when it occurs within those struggles. Women's liberation is but a part of a larger anti-imperialist struggle: it is through supporting—and emulating—black and Vietnamese men that women will be liberated.

First of all, Weatherman's influence over B&R is shown by the fact that two-thirds of this article of dissent from Weathercocksmanship is spent discussing imperialism and racism. (Racism does exist among women and among feminists, but it is not racism that has forced *all* women into an inferior role.) B&R complains that the revolutionary commitment of women in Weatherman is "measured by male chauvinist standards; they must struggle in terms defined by men," but the entire paper has been assuming propriety of Weatherman's priorities.

B&R does make some acute observations about women's position in the movement. The word movement when used by B&R always means the New Left, not the Women's Liberation Movement. One instance is a quote picked up from an article written for *Leviathan* (by Kathy McAfee and Myrna Wood) in 6/69:

> Many of the characteristics which one needs in order to become respected in the movement—like the ability to argue loud and fast and aggressively and to excel in the 'I'm more revolutionary than you' style of debate—are traits which our society consistently cultivates in men and discourages in women from childhood. But these traits are neither inherently male nor universally human: rather they are particularly appropriate to a brutally competitive society.

The position paper continues right on:

> The Weatherman position on monogamy illustrates how women are delegitimitized individually and collectively. The women's movement has been very critical of the present institution of the nuclear family . . . our analysts tell us that an attack on the effects of the nuclear family must be an attack on its material basis socially and politically—and not dependent on individual solution.
>
> The key to ending the nuclear family as a prescriptive institution is to end women's oppression and discrimination in the *entire* society.
>
> Weatherman has chosen to ignore this complex oppression, and instead decreed the end of monogamy within their collectives, with very destructive consequences . . . i.e., they believe an individual woman can will herself to be different, which ignores the social reality that women's pressure for monogamy grew from their unequal position in the entire society (in the home, at work, and in the movement). It is interesting that Weatherman chose to deal with monogamy rather

than nuclear families. Such emphasis does not deal collectively with the daily pressures—like children—that most women face. (Instead children become the woman's full-time problem and responsibility again—thus guaranteeing that only a small elite of young women without families could ever participate in Weatherman struggles.)

Weathermen stress cutting off all personal ties and responsibilities. This model may be a relief to the men—freeing them from emotional involvement and responsibility. But it is liberating for neither men nor women.

In the last two paragraphs, B&R writes:

> We believe that women must make revolutions for themselves as well as other people. Women's oppression has been ignored and used by other socialist movements before. There is no reason why women should allow this to happen in America, now.
>
> Yet, we also realize that this only indicates the problems for the women's movement—and does not pretend to answer finally the question of how *we* can fight racism and imperialism as part of the fight for our own liberation.[12]

Nowhere in this B&R paper can one find the single-minded concentration on women's issues that an examination of early feminism shows to be the necessary precondition for radical change in the condition of women. Ultimately BREAD AND ROSES is a feminist group, sometimes cogently, but as often as not apologetically.

The other well-known group in the Boston area is Women's Liberation in Somerville, formerly called Cell 16. This group received a hostile and distorted press. All articles discussing Cell 16 came with photographs of some member of the group in full karate garb, practicing a chop. The group now seeks to avoid publicity. They demand a two-point program for all women: 1) Free full-time child-care centers, day and night, and 2) free self-defense instruction for all women.

The group publishers *No More Fun & Games.* This journal is one of the best published in the movement. It consists of poetry, art, short stories and radical analysis of women's oppression that is at once thoughtful and provocative.

The word is going around in the women's movement, as a proof of the dissemination of the ideas on female liberation, of the reputed existence in Bloomington, Indiana, of a communal house of single parents, all women, living and working out their problems together. According to their representative, WOMEN'S LIBERATION IN BLOOMINGTON consists of "various action groups within the movement . . . attempting to make structural changes in legal, educational, occupational, and family institutions." Among the projects of the group are a cooperative day-care center, fighting for better employment opportunities and conditions and establishing a women's liberation house and central meeting place.

The group hopes that its members will, "by relating meaningfully to one another, help each other resolve the inner conflicts they confront when they try to break away from the traditional women's roles."

In America there now exist women's liberation groups from Albuquerque to Seattle and from San Francisco to Baltimore. The movement on the west coast is highly diversified. It has been estimated that there are perhaps a thousand women in the movement in the San Francisco-Berkeley area alone. The political alliances in the metropolitan area are roughly East Bay: Berkeley, women students, political activists, socialists, and West Bay: San Francisco and Palo Alto. Oakland has only a few feminists who travel to either the East or West Bay organizations. There is communication between the East and West Bay group, but in general, once again there is evident the familiar divide between women who are still allied with the male Left and women who give women's rights sole priority. In September, the women's movement set up a central headquarters at the Wesleyan Foundation Church. All women's groups in the Bay Area can meet and work out of this center.

The Bay Area has several newsletters: *Tooth and Nail* has been described as a conglomerate of information, literature representing every position in the WL Movement. It declares itself the Bay Area Women's Liberation Journal.

There is also another more programmatic sheet put out by Berkeley WL This newsletter announces meetings and occurrences within the Berkeley activist women's movement. Feminism is one of their interests.

An organization of all the women's rights collectives in northern California is presently under discussion. This would provide more coordination on projects and research and communication among the groups in northern California. The Bay area movement is slowly reorganizing and revaluing its goals due to the deterioration it suffered after the August convention on women's rights.

The Women's Liberation Movement is rapidly gaining adherents and stimulating women to a reconsideration of the nature of womanhood.

Chapter 2

The Relationship of Black Women to the Women's Liberation Movement

The Women's Liberation Movement is a multitude of white women with an only occasional black sister to lend color to the meetings. At this point in American history there are many forces divisive of black-white political coalitions, but the oppression of women has induced rivalries that intensify these separations.

Any analysis of the current hostility and/or indifference to feminism among black women must begin with a consideration of the old reality of black imitation of whites and the resulting self-contempt. In ways subtle and obvious, our society socializes women into narcissism. Fashion magazines tout the desirable woman much as advertisements glorify the high-salaried man. Girls soon learn to rate themselves according to their desirability to boys and men.

Black society has patterned itself closely on white people, but since blackness connotes ugliness and evil to whites, black women have been despised as coarse and animal-like in their sensuality. They have been despised both by whites and by their own people.

Under slavery blacks learned to value, revere even, white aesthetics and the white ethos. They soon learned that the slaves who most closely imitated whites in language, manners and, most importantly, looks, were favored by the masters. "Part-white children sold for more than black children. They used them for house girls," reminisced an ex-slave.[1] House work was considerably easier than field work and the house servants and concubines thought themselves better than the "field niggers." Indeed where it pleased the master to assert his power by keeping those slaves most like himself for his pleasure and leisure hours, many benefits came to them.

After abolition, these lighter-skinned ex-slaves maintained their ascendancy in the wage-earning world. Being better educated, they were more likely to acquire advanced educations and enter the professional fields. Forming an elite, they sometimes lived in their own towns in the South, and darker-skinned blacks were unwelcome. They had separate churches, clubs, and social customs that closely imitated those of white society.

A dark-skinned man who became successful would seek one of the light-skinned elites to solidify his status. Caucasoid features as the visible badge of respectability and worthiness were admired as blacks sought to become as white as possible. A good complexion was a light skin. Good hair was straight or curly, but never kinky. Black was bad; black was ugly.

As late as the mid-1960's, black sororities in the South were known to reject prospective pledges for their dark complexions. Sometimes dark-skinned girls already in sororities would blackball dark-skinned pledges. All blacks rejected their own blackness. Consequently, color-conscious was a frequent epithet; dark-skinned people watched lighter-skinned people closely for signs of rejection, and they often didn't have to look very hard. Robbed of their culture and deprived of their identity, the pre-civil rights movement blacks sought to escape their awful blackness, stigma of their fall from grace. Black militance is a healthy effort to reclaim the black man's rightful self-acceptance and identity.

The black middle class has not joined the militant movement. As a class, it has closely identified itself with white America. Up until now it has been a conservative force in the black community. This middle class, largely descended from the lighter-skinned slaves, has been the segment of black society that has benefited most from things as they are. They have preferred the advantages they know to the mere possibilities of the black revolution.

Black bourgeois women are the most closely mimetic of all blacks. In black culture, they have been the almost-desirable ones. Their conventionality usually demands the full panoply of middle-class acquisitions. They are the perfect consumers, and as such, the perfect mates for ambitious black men.

Ebony magazine advertises in *The New York Times* that the black bourgeoisie is a more avaricious consumer class than whites with comparable incomes. Of course in black families, as in all American families, the wife is the high priestess of consumption. However, as black families entertain more in their homes (they are uncertain of their welcome in places of public entertainment), wives bear a larger responsibility for creating a sheltering environment.

At a time when middle-class white youths are rebelling against parental mores and ethics, the young black bourgeoises continue in their passion for propriety. While some young black males are to be seen in the bohemian ghettos, black females are rare, and middle-class black females even rarer. It is seldom that you will find a college-educated black girl living with her boyfriend. Black girls believe, and not without some cause, that middle-class black males don't marry black females who have been promiscuous.

Not surprisingly, these young, almost entirely conservative black women have seldom joined the Women's Liberation Movement, for they are usually apolitical. They constitute that part of the black community that has remained the longest outside the mainstream of the sixties. It is as if their mimetic interaction with the white community were located back in the fifties. Many black bourgeois families disapprove of the Afro hairdo. Black women of Katharine Cleaver's background are rarely seen in public life. Middle-class black women remain in the home, in the private lives of the community.

Even more rarely encountered than bourgeoises in women's liberation are poor black women. Lower-class black women have joined the black militant movement so it is not that they are apolitical. Furthermore the Black Panthers are considered the vanguard of Leftist politics in America, and all female liberation groups profess empahty with blacks as a kindred oppressed group. It is remarkable then that feminists often cite the political strategy of the black movement and encourage themselves with black precedents while they are seemingly unable to attract black women to the female liberation cause.

One reason that women's liberation doesn't or won't attract black women is that blacks are suspicious of whites who might coopt their support, energy and drive. Feminists are perceived as whites before they are seen to be oppressed. Secondly, black lower-class women are presently emphasizing their independence of, and prideful difference from, white women. Thirdly, poor black women are too occupied struggling for essentials: shelter, food and clothing to organize themselves around the issue of women's rights.

Fourthly, lower-class black women have deliberately submerged their identities in the struggle for racial equality. This is in tune with the collective spirit of the sixties. In black radical politics, individual concerns are superseded by the needs of the group or party. In this context, it is possible to view an autonomous women's drive for rights as an obstacle to radical changes. Black feminism would thus be another attempt by the power structure to divide black men and women. Feminist goals, like abortion on demand and easily obtainable birth control, are viewed with paranoid suspicion by some black militants at a time when they are literally fighting for their lives and looking everywhere to increase their numbers.

Lower-class black women have received little satisfaction from the identities allowed them by society, which were the identities based on close imitation of whites, a charade at which they were pre-destined to fail. Joining the Women's Liberation Movement may seem at this time like a re-entry into the old farce of pretending to be white. They are therefore not drawn by the feminists' cry for self-determination. Rather, they seek black militant movements, whether male-dominated or female and organized around specific grievances such as housing, for the self-respect and pride through group identity that they offer.

To women's liberation groups, marriage and the family are the roots of women's oppression, while to black women of the middle class, this thought is abhorrent, and to black lower-class women, their oppression is completely racial. Yet black women are the largest and most oppressed minority group in the United States. Their oppression by whites is clearly discernible, but their oppression by men is not recognizable to most people.

In the past, the analogy between the oppression of slaves and the oppression of women was easily seen. Nineteenth-century feminists had only to substitute the word wife for the word slave to understand the nature of man's tyranny over woman. The nineteenth-century woman had no redress against a husband who wasted her property, consorted with other women, beat her and beat their children and she could easily empathize with female slaves. As Maria Child wrote in *An Appeal in Favour of the Class of Americans Called Africans:* "(the slave) is the property of her master, and her daughters are his property. . . . They must be entirely subservient to the will of their owner, on pain of being whipped as near unto death as will comport with his interest, or quite to death if it suit his pleasure." As Andrew Sinclair makes clear: "Any woman who feared rape herself could identify with the female slave and transfer her hatred from the plantation owner to the whole male sex. . . . In that way then, the wrongs inflicted on Negro women were the wrongs of woman-kind."²

Today the oppression of women is more subtly prosecuted. Without consciousness-raising, the ways in which they are controlled are generally unclear to women. Moreover the inferior position of women is of such long tradition that it has remained unquestioned even by radical thinkers, that is by male radical thinkers.

Just as black militants expect black women to sink their abilities into the movement and fulfill their interests by fighting for racial equality, so abolitionists demanded that nineteenth-century feminists turn away from the "woman question" lest they harm the fight to free the slaves. The Grimke sisters who linked the fight for women's rights with the anti-slavery fight were told they could most benefit humanity by working against slavery. This is really social feminism: the idea that it is woman's duty to be selflessly enrolled in working for a higher cause. Certainly Theodore Weld's accusation to Angelina Grimke might well come from the mouths of black nationalists or other blacks who see black women's problems only as the result of the economic position of black men.

"Your woman's rights! You put the cart before the horse; you drag the tree by the top in attempting to push your *woman's* rights until human rights have gone ahead and broken the *path*," declared Mr. Weld.

Angelina Grimke's answer might well be used by black women today if black race is substituted for slave. "The slave may be freed and woman be where she is, but woman can not be freed and the slave remain where he is."³

It is not only militants who ignore the black woman's right to self-determination. Dorothy Height, President of the National Council of Negro Women, has said: "Negro women have the same problems and hopes as other women, but they cannot take the same things for granted." Her analysis then led her to the same arguments as those voiced by the abolitionists in accusing woman's rights of putting the cart before the horse: "If the Negro woman has a major underlying concern, it is the status of the Negro man and his position in the community and his need for feeling himself an important person, free and able to make his contribution in the whole society in order that he may strengthen his home."[4] Mrs. Height's analysis, like that of the black radicals, stops short of the inequities between men and women. Black men doubtless see women's oppression as inconsequential compared to blacks' sufferings.

Black women have the same needs for self-determination as all people have. They have been made to feel some guilt at the thought of acting in their own interests rather than in those of their race, where these seem to diverge in the minds of black males. The inferior position of women is not due to economics or race; otherwise, in socialist countries, or in racially homogeneous countries, women would enjoy a functional equality and not just improved status. The real basis of the oppression of women is man's psychological need for dominance. Men need women to make them feel good. A typical remark from an untypically honest male is: "If women weren't weaker than men, I'd just as soon sleep with men." As Gore Vidal, among many, has commented, sexual congress is a power relationship.

The rejection of black women by black men is a phenomenon best explained by the need to dominate that underlies male-female relations. As such, this rejection is an excellent study for feminists. The strength of the resistance to women's independence is shown by the strong epithets directed against black women. The black male's reaction is the forerunner of what all feminists will face as they grow in strength. As women begin to assume positions of equality with men, they will meet virulent abuse, much like that endured by black women now. They will also discover that men will reject them for more "feminine" women.

Black sociologist Calvin Hernton's *Sex and Racism*

in America is filled with examples of the defamation and rejection now subtle, now blatant, that are the lot of black women. For example: "It is no mystery why white society is now tending to accept the black woman more readily than the black male. First of all, the Negro woman, like the white woman, does not represent to the white world as much of an aggressor against the present power structure as does the Negro man." It hasn't been true any time in the sixties that black women were hired before black men. On the contrary black women got little benefit from the drive to find black talent.

The rare black woman who has achieved a position of prominence was bitterly resented by black males. Black personnel men have been known to lose the résumés of promising black women. One such administrator at a famous radio and television station told a black woman applicant: "We already have enough sisters in the communications industry. It's time the brothers got ahead."

"In the executive talent shortage of the 1960's, some organizations encouraged women in the patronizing way they had encouraged promotable Negroes when the Negro rights movement was popular, but the efforts to see that qualified women were promoted were much more half-hearted than those promoting Negroes. In 1967, for instance, 15% of a group of companies queried by the Bureau of National Affairs said they had undertaken aggrressive recruiting of promotable Negroes in response to Title VII, but only one company reported an aggressive policy of recruiting women.

" 'I'm not ready for a woman,' a frank management consultant confessed in 1966 when a woman executive recommended a woman for a job he had open. 'But boy, would I love to get hold of a good Negro!' "[5] In the business world, sex is more of a barrier than race.

Another example from Mr. Hernton's book is: "When it comes to women, the Negro male, like the white male, is a product and victim of male supremacy, and he becomes disgruntled and difficult to get along with when 'his women' are in a position where they no longer have to honor his claim to superiority. In addition to the crisis occurring in contemporary race relations, a more specific crisis is ensuing in the relations between Negro men and Negro women—and I suspect it will become more intense as time goes on unless Negro women (I say women because, in this regard, I doubt the capacity of the men) to initiate measures to resolve it.'"

What he is doing here, other than lightly criticizing male supremacists, is to place on women the burden and full responsibility for reconciling their achievements with male vanity. He cagily ends the chapter at this point without suggesting just what she is to sacrifice to this peacemaking mission. Men such as Hernton believe that women alone can save the human race through their superior virtues. Doubtless he is opposed to the oppression of women, but he would object to full equality for them as likely to bring them down to the level of men.

Yet history has made black women more independent than most American women. "Although the African matriarchal pattern" (actually not a true matriarchy as only lineage was traced through the mother, and authority and disciplinary powers were invested in the mother's brother) "had been largely destroyed, slave life itself gave the Negro woman a unique status. It was not only that, in the constant flux of slave relations, her relationship to the children was clear while the father's was often not, but also, that, in addition to her capacity as a worker, the owner profited from her child-bearing and rearing her young. She was, therefore, less apt to be sold out of hand than the male and was the more stable element in what little there was of slave family life.

"As a rule, the Negro woman as wife and mother was the mistress of her cabin, and, save for the interference of the overseer, her wishes in regard to mating and family matters were paramount. Neither economic necessity nor tradition had instilled in her the spirit of subordination to masculine authority."'

Because of this failure to develop subserviency to the male black women are belittled by both middle- and lower-class black men. The middle-class black man, such as Mr. Hernton, sees the black woman as domineering and castrating. To wit: "Repeatedly I have witnessed Negro women virtually dominating their white husbands. There may be fights, but she capitalizes on her Negroness and on her sex image by wielding a sort of *Amazon mastery* (italics mine) over the white male. In all but a few black woman–white man relationships, it is the man who must do the adjusting —and what he must adjust to is nothing less than what is referred to as the Negro's mode of existence or the Negro's conceptualization of life in the United States.""

Mr. Hernton is displaying common anxieties and fears in his emotionally charged statement about the "Amazon mastery" that he says black women develop over their white husbands. His translation of circumstantial necessity into a deliberate attempt at oppression ignores social realities: Discrimination and intolerance invariably force interracial couples to live in black communities, or at least in well-integrated ones.

The lower-class black male sees black women as bitches. The welfare check has made the poor black woman economically independent of the men who come and go in her life, and on whom she cannot rely. Poor black males complain of being told to "Get out! And don't bring your ass back here until you've got a job!" There is antagonism between black males and females, especially in the poorest segments of the community. The women are contemptuous of the men for not being able to keep jobs, or not being able to find work and provide for their families, or for throwing their money away on gambling, other women, and drinking. The women belittle the men for not taking

84

care of business. The men curse the women for not being feminine and comforting.

The mistake that sociologists are making and that black men seem to be making is the assumption that these women have chosen to be heads of their families. They have become heads of households by default—as the only responsible adults in their families. It is interesting to note that the state menaces and subordinates these women in much the same way that the salary-earning male head of the household does his wife. Protection has its price.

It is the pressures of poverty and slum life that grind down the black family and destroy the role of the black male as father-protector. It is these pressures, not black women, that make the confidence man the ghetto hero. In Harlem, in Watts, in Hough, the admired man beats the game: dresses sharp, has a string of girlfriends, and doesn't have a steady job. He gets by doing a little of this and a little of that. For the poor black man, there is no ego aggrandizement in the traditional role of head of the house. Economic and social racism force him to be inadequate in such a role. And so the black bitch was created to justify the confidence man.

"A dark-skinned woman is discriminated against by Negroes as well as whites. 'A yellow woman may be low-down, but a black one is evil,' goes the saying among Negroes. She is not born evil but her chances of being genteel, loving, and personable are virtually impossible in a world that sees nothing but her color. Here Mr. Hernton is actually concurring in the existence of the mythical black bitch.

To continue: "This is why many black women in the North have developed what I call 'black woman chauvinism.' They have a genuine hatred for white women and the Negro men who pursue them; they hate the sight of a light-skinned Negro woman. After all, black women are females, and they have the desires that all females have—for attention, for sexual gratification, for respect, for reverence, for sexual self-esteem. And if they do not realize such desires, like any other women, they tend to become 'difficult personalities,' 'evil'."[9] Black women are evil, and it's understandable that they should be, says Hernton. He assumes that women are estimable to the extent that they can attract men. Obviously these women are pitiable, perhaps contemptible because of their lack of allure.

Abbey Lincoln, according to Fletcher Knebel, first verbalized the current black female unrest (it is as yet unorganized) in the face of this kind of rejection. "We are the women," she declared, ". . . whose nose is 'too big,' whose mouth is 'too big and loud,' whose behind is 'too big and broad,' whose feet are 'too big and flat,' whose face is 'too black and shiny' . . . who's just too damned much for everybody." She was referring to Sapphire, the Amazon of the black male imagination.

Implied by Mr. Hernton's book is the failure of black women to sustain black men. By their own involvement with being black, black women have not been able to take the nurturing role that men look for in women. "The point is that many of the darker Negro men who pursue white mates do so because their own women have rejected them because they are 'black and ugly'. . . . Whereas white women . . . can live with a so-called 'black and ugly' Negro without constantly making the Negro secretly despise himself for the way he happens to look . . . Thus we hear some Negro men proclaiming that such and such a white woman treats them better than the females of their own race."[10] He adds parenthetically that the same applies to Negro women, but obviously their needs are secondary. Once again women are being valued for their ability to make men happy.

Further bias is evident in Mr. Hernton's conclusion that "The deeper meaning in the practice of Negro women in the South of beating their children (especially boys) to a point of sheer exhaustion is to be found somewhere in the pent-up rage that black women have in their hearts against white women and against a sociosexual morality that denies black women the right to be beautiful, loving and idealized by black and white men alike."[11] This practice of excessive punishment of their children by Southern (usually) blacks is capable of at least two other interpretations.

One: the authors of *Black Rage,* William Grier and Price Cobbs, theorized that black mothers punished and demoralized their male children to make them subservient to whites. The mothers did this for the survival of their children. Two: It is not only the mother who beats the children in the Southern family, the father also figures in accounts as an administrator of the razor strap. This refers of course to the generation of fathers and mothers, now in their late forties and fifties, whose own parents were the children and grandchildren of former slaves. The customary brutality of slave beatings, the fear, expectation and acceptance of them, has become part of the psychic building blocks of the black family.

Listen to these accounts from ex-slaves:

"His (the master's) wife or children could git mad with you, and if they told him anything they always beat you. Most times he beat slaves when they had done nothing a-tall. . . . He put her in what us called the swing, and beat her till she couldn't holler. . . . Whenever your master had you swinging up, nobody wouldn't take you down. Sometimes a man would help his wife, but most times he was beat afterwards."

"Before my father (the master) gave me to his sister, I was tied and strapped and whipped like a beast by my father, till I was unconscious, and then he left me strapped to a tree all night in cold and rainy weather. . . . When Missy took that bell offen me, I think I in Heaven 'cause I could lie down and go to sleep. When I did I couldn't wake up for a long time, and when I did wake up I'd be scared to death I'd see my father with his whip and that old bell."

"When he go to whip a nigger he make him strip to the waist and take a cat-o'-nine-tails and bring the blisters, and then bust the blister with a wide strap of leather fastened to a stick handle. I seen the blood running outen man's back, all the way from the neck to the waist."

"Many times a nigger git blistered and cut up so that we have to git a sheet and grease it with lard and wrap 'em up in it, and they have to wear a greasy cloth wrapped around they body under the shirt for three-four days after they git a big whipping."[12]

It is not unlikely that people used to such treatment would beat their children to discipline them.

The distortions that underlie the transformation of the black mother into a witchlike figure with magical powers to destroy are obviously found in the educated as well as the ignorant. In a recent quote a black educator said: "For the black man, the black woman is too much like his mother. He sees her as domineering, bossy, a woman who runs things. He wants a desirable, easy sex companion, and he finds her in the white woman." What will happen when this desirable doll becomes a real woman? Perhaps she will be rejected for an easygoing Oriental?

An admissions official at Columbia University criticizes black women in these terms: "Too often black American women fail to free themselves from the psychological impediments imposed by their overprotective mothers. As a result, they fail to develop the self-confidence and self-assuredness necessary to achieve full womanhood in a market where the company of the black male is becoming more and more competitive."

"We kind of *fear* (italics mine) the middle-class black girl we meet around school. She's snobbish, uppity and inclined to sneer at a black man unless he excels at something. White girls, for a lot of reasons, are easier, less Victorian, and let's face it, they have their own money."

It is the fear and anxiety of the black male that lead to the construction of the "evil" black female. By now, the superstructure of the "black bitch" bears as little relation to the real black woman as any myth to the reality. The preceding quotes suggest that the men speaking have no honest contact with women of either race. The magical approach of the male to the female is an ancient orientation toward women as the aliens of the human world.

The complaint that black women challenge black men is further proof of the threatening nature of female independence to most men. Philip Roth's indictment of the Jewish mother may soon seem mild as black men achieve more power. It seems significant that the literature of the omnipotent Jewish mother with her all-devouring love has become a familiar theme of our literature just as the Jews have been assimilated into the power centers of American life. Although the parallels in the black and Jewish traditions are slight, both cultures are now remarkable for the vehemence of the attack on their women. I suggest that black literature will increasingly consist of virulent attacks on the evil black mother as black men move into positions of power.

When black men attain power and approximate the status of the white male of the higher classes, they tend to reject their own women for not conforming to WASP standards of femininity. Black women and Jewish women are being fitted to the Procrustean bed of the WASP female's behavior and personality.

"Uppity Women Unite" is a motto of the Women's Liberation Movement. As all women achieve self-determination, white women will cease to be preferred. The power conflict that informs sexual congress will be revealed, as condemnations of women as castrating, aggressive, snobbish, uppity, difficult and evil rise from men. But black women are still captive to the idea that to be attractive to men is the only way to be a fine woman. They are still dependent on men for feelings of self-worth.

The new black man (I'm black, and I'm proud!) is certainly attractive to white women. His defiance has made him a compelling figure. Still his self-acceptance is often only superficial. It is still possible to hear remarks such as this one made by two dashiki-clad youths, as Miss Black Teenage America went by: "Why did they have to choose someone so black?" Such men and boys choose white women out of self-loathing. Any white skin is better than any black one. Surprisingly enough, these attitudes can be found in quite sophisticated men: Afro heads and processed minds.

The black civil rights movement of the sixties, with its growing militancy and heightened racial self-confidence, generated a rejection of the self-hatred projected onto black people in America. Suddenly black is beautiful. Black is beautiful, and your (black) bird can sing. Black women were asked to legitimize the motto that Black Is Beautiful by wearing their hair natural and adopting African clothes, and, it was implied, by only dating black men. Black women were even told not to wear pants. Naturalism, in the minds of many, became confused with a return to a world defined and ruled by men. Some black men wish, by becoming militant, to assume the powers of white men in an earlier, simpler century.

In the age of the Organization Man and middle-class anonymity, some black men would be supermales. Their aggressiveness identifies them as such to themselves and to white females. The white female sees the black male as he wishes to be seen—that is, as far as his public presentation goes.

Black men pursue white women not simply as the

90

most beautiful women and easy, but also as the symbols of the white man's privileges. White women and black women have been accepting this without criticism, but now black women are becoming increasingly vocal in their anger at this manipulation. Most white women still are not aware of the nature of black man's desire for them.

To feminists, the male aggressive attitude that a woman is to sleep with as a hole is to dig is objectionable. Many of the phrases used in slang indicate that women are seen as objects: "gash," "pussy," and "cunt." The black man is the chief victim of this supermale psychology. He accepts the myth as projected onto him, plays the part and is irresistible to white women.

Black men often can date white women who wouldn't have anything to do with them if they had the same personal characteristics but were white. Their blackness immediately makes them the peak of masculinity. Those white females who prefer black males say that white males don't even know how to smile at you; they don't know how to rap; they act as if they don't know what a woman is for! They like black life—the blues life, the jazz tradition. Dating black men, they have all the advantages (glamor) of blackness and elude the oppression.

Black women are chiefly angered by black men's pursuit of white women without understanding it. Fletcher Knebel quoted a letter from a black woman to *Ebony:* "I, as a black woman, realize that our men have been brainwashed to believe their women are nothing, but just as they are being awakened to the fact that they are beautiful, why can't they also be taught how to treat us? Our men seem to feel that as part of the black, we are beautiful, but as women, they don't even really see us."

"Many black women who saw the Broadway hit *The Great White Hope,* came away depressed," noted Mr. Knebel. "They could not forget that the play's real Jack Johnson, once the world's heavyweight champion, found no solace in black women, and that he had three white wives. Nor could they forget that Jones (who acted Jack Johnson), had himself married a white woman."

Mr. Knebel's assumption that woman is to solace man is, of course, unacceptable, but what is more depressing is the black women's self-castigation because Jack Johnson had married white women. As the play clearly shows, Johnson treated his wives badly, and his having *three* indicates the difficulties of living with him. These women are wounded by a conception of women as successful only if they have husbands.

Women of both races are being manipulated by their fear of losing or of never winning a husband. The anxiety to please and to be nice to men, to make them feel good, is inculcated on females from infancy and increasingly forced on them as they enter puberty.

The results of this are sexual jealousy and envy among women. All over New York, there have been actual battles between white women and black women over black men. Usually this sexual hostility is soft-pedaled, but whether it is spoken or silent, it is a poor background for black-white coalition in the feminist movement.

New York radio station WBAI's Julius Lester states very calmly that if he dies an unnatural death, it will probably be at the hands of a black woman enraged by his having a white wife.

A recent forum at the N.Y.U. Law School is indicative of the amount of resentment between the races. Fannie Lou Hamer and some friends of hers, well-wishers and supporters, had been invited to speak to law school students. Also invited were three women from the Women's Liberation Movement in New York City. After the feminists told something about the aims and purpose of women's liberation, the meeting was thrown open for questions from the audience.

The black women in the audience, most of whom were supporters of Fannie Lou Hamer, although some

92

were law students, dominated the discussion period. Their first question was: "How many black women are there in the Women's Liberation Movement?" The answer, Not many, but we are working to reach more, was met by: "That's right! because black women aren't sick. Black women don't hate sex. You white women don't know how to make a man happy!" "White women can't cook." "You hate men!" The feeling grew even stronger after that. Most of the audience seemed incapable of listening to what the feminists had to say, but it was the black women who crystallized the fear and resentment by giving it a racist slant.

Some black men date and marry white women because they have fallen in love with particular individuals, but on the street, it is difficult to distinguish these men from the black men who reject any black woman as ugly. Also white women sometimes flaunt their black men as prizes they have won in the competition with black women.

The sexual competition between black and white women will diminish as women learn to value themselves as people, independent of their relationships to men. White women will not then be flattered by the pursuit of black men when these men only see in them the appanage of white power; nor will black women panic and feel betrayed at the sight of black men with white women.

Black women find in the black movement the collective identity of the sixties. Women's liberation has offered them nothing like this. The black movement is so gratifying to these newly realized needs for group pride that black women have stayed in the black movement despite many injustices. Women in black, radical organizations have sometimes found that they are constitutionally barred from holding office. If they are elected to office, they are figureheads. The Black Panthers have hitherto allowed women little significant voice in strategy and communications. But the Panther men are now often in jails or in graveyards and, for the first time in many chapters, women are now as prominent as men. This is due to an emergent situation much as in any country in time of war. But Panther membership comes largely from the poorest segments of the ghettos—those people to whom no white radical movement offers any hope or self-acceptance. A young woman organizing a Black Panther free breakfast program for children was not surprised when her two male assistants said that she should cook the breakfasts and do the dishes while they should rap to the children. She countered strongly by reversing the roles, but she succeeded only with difficulty, and expects the resistance to keep recurring on other questions.

Black militant politics offers women association with men as women's liberation does not. The black male, newly proud and assertive of his ability to take care of his women, is saying with you behind me, we'll win; and when we do, you'll be my queen, my better half, my lady on a pedestal. Through black power, you'll get the white woman's status (and the black male will win dominance over the female).

Few black women speak up in public for the woman's right to control her own body, but few of the black women who are best informed about, and most familiar with, the pill and the diaphragm are in the black radical movement.

College-age black women have been actively involved in the actions on campus, but again they have taken the traditional feminine role. In the takeover at Cornell, it was a source of pride to black male students to protect the girls who had been threatened and abused by some of the white fraternity men on campus. These same girls wound up frying chicken for the boys at the barricades.

A reliable source in the Harvard Organization of Black Unity (OBU) asserts that whenever a black girl becomes too articulate and aggressive at the meetings, a boy from the group is assigned to seduce her, and then, as his conquest, keep her in a more traditional position within the organization.

It will be interesting to see if the black female graduates of this year's campus actions will be willing to breed for black power. It is not unlikely that five years from now a wave of lower-class and college-educated black women, disillusioned by their oppression in the black militant movement (much like the white women from radical student organizations in feminism now) will be coming into the feminist movement.

While the black militant movement offers black women and black men a proud group identity, women's liberation works for abortion and equal opportunities for hiring and advancement, which the black woman sees as already having cost her black men. While it will soon no longer be true, in 1965, more black women had attended college and held college degrees than black males. It left the black college-educated woman without a man of similar background. Emphasis has been placed on winning the men education and middle-class employment, but this has been urged at the expense of the women. Black women have been urged to step back and let the men catch up. Originally black women were given more education to give them the chance for employment away from predatory white men. Black women working as domestics, particularly in the South, were invariably subject to and had little protection from the advances of male employers and of other men in the town. By educating girls in the family to higher status, the black family was acting to protect them from this.

Black women have special problems that women's liberation has not focused on. The percent of black women in the labor force has always been higher than that of whites. In 1900, 41% of black women were employed as compared with 17% of whites. In 1963, black women still made up 25% more of the female working force than did white. About two-thirds of black women workers are in the lowest paid service occupations.

These women are not usually covered by social security, medical insurance or disability or old-age benefits. The President's Commission on the Status of Women urged the federal government to take further steps to enforce compliance with the law requiring social security for these women and to educate the Negro household worker on her rights and benefits under this program.

Black women generally want to move up out of their low-status, and thus undesirable, occupations as domestics. Women's liberation should concentrate in helping the generation of women now trapped in these jobs by working to upgrade skills in these jobs to the professional level and by improving employment conditions. Furthermore, as few Americans can afford to pay domestic workers a good salary on a full-time basis, domestic work should be reorganized to be done by contractors—professional workers would arrive in the home at the stipulated time to do the contracted duties, which would be clearly delineated and enforced. Modern equipment and training would be given the domestic professionals with certificates awarded on completion of studies.

Such a program would be a two-fold benefit. All housewives could be freed of this task which is particularly onerous for the working woman, who is usually held responsible for keeping the household as well.

There should also be training available for domestic professionals to move into other fields when they desire.

Black and Puerto Rican women are often trapped in domestic or factory jobs because they are barred from white-collar jobs. According to a report of the President's Commission on the Status of Women: "A major means of entering the secretarial field is through graduation from a recognized business or secretarial school. Many of these schools, however, do not admit Negroes.

Yet they are granted licenses to operate and have such advantages as tax exemption and indirect federal funds through veterans' programs." Women's liberation has not focused its energies on these problems of minority women.

In 1964, white men who worked full time earned a median income of $6,497; black men $4,285; white women $3,859; and black women $2,674. In 1960, 44% of black married women with children under six years old were working full-time. The children of these mothers are often not cared for properly during their mother's working hours. Women's liberation should press for an enormous increase in community child-care facilities.

Women's liberation has directed itself to the impediments to the aspirations of college-educated women. There was an outcry against this at the northeastern Congress to Unite Women. A great many of the 3.8 million illiterate women in the United States are non-white. Adult education programs and vocational training programs suitable for the uneducated woman should become priorities of women's liberation if it is to attract black and Puerto Rican women.

Statistics have shown that proportionately more black women are heads of families than whites. "The tendency (for black families to be matriarchal) has continued because of the inability of many Negro men to get a decent job and earn a sufficient wage to carry their responsibilities of family life. Thus the Negro wife is forced into the labor market where she often earns more than her husband and sometimes becomes the only earner for the family. Therefore, not by choice, she may become the head of the household. Because of the barriers to education and better-paying jobs encountered by men, the Negro woman frequently has had to assume additional social and economic burdens."

Scant attention has been paid in women's liberation to problems of women who head households.

Minority women have other problems that receive little attention in the movement. In a recent article in *The New York Times,* Paul Montgomery wrote: "A study of births in New York City in 1967 showed that 5.3% of births among whites were illegitimate . . . The figures for blacks were 24 per cent in 1957 and 38.3 per cent in 1967, and for Puerto Ricans 10.7 per cent in 1957 and 21.9 per cent in 1967. For Central Harlem in 1967, the illegitimacy rate was 54.2 per cent." While women's liberation is working for the right to abortion on demand, illegitimate birth rates among New York Puerto Ricans doubled within a decade. More than half of the children born in Central Harlem are illegitimate, yet women's liberation has not spoken to the problems of unwed mothers. Furthermore it has been noted that "while few white unwed mothers keep their babies, two-thirds of black and Puerto Rican mothers do." There is a welfare rights organization, dominated by black women with a few Puerto Ricans, but this organization remains outside the women's liberation group.

There has been no effort from within the movement to work on these issues. There is a nascent black women's liberation group, formed as a caucus of the welfare rights organization, on the Lower East Side. Hopefully this group will confront the problems of single-parenthood. Women's liberation has generally left the minorities to deal with their particular problems themselves. This, then, is the explanation of why there are few minority women in feminism.

Black and white women can work together for women's liberation if the movement changes its priorities to work on issues that affect the lives of minority-group women. If raised consciousness shows white women that black men are pursuing them as symbols of white achievements; if black women currently in the black radical movement in the cities and on campus become disillusioned with their oppression by the Left; if women are educated to value themselves for their independent identities; if women of both races see their problems as originating in female dependency on men and in their self-contempt, then women will make a revolution in our social and economic order.

Chapter 3

Analysis of Contemporary Feminism

The Women's Liberation Movement arose out of the redefinitions of politics that hallmarked the 60's. The new politics is a demand to determine not just the specifics of participation in the establishment of government but to determine the relationship of the individual to the people and institutions of our society. Politics is no longer regarded as the business of voting for candidates. Politics is now the art of determining how one's life will be lived and implementation of freedom in the presentation of self in everyday life.

It is significant that the first autonomous organization of the WL Movement was formed at the Conference for New Politics. WL shares the vocabulary, political strategies, and certain of its factions give total acceptance to the philosophical underpinnings of the New Left. The new politicians of the 60's, having read Marcuse, Brown, Laing, Hesse and Cleaver, focused their energies on forming a society in which it is possible for the integrated self of the individual to develop and function. Determined not to grow up absurd, they developed the vocabulary of alienation and sought out the authentic in experience. Still this search was reserved for the men of the New Left.

Women's liberation groups first formed as caucuses of male political groups. The women in the groups, which were usually liberal or radical organizations, discovered that radical analysis of the male-female relationship, a necessary step in the self-determination of women, was never undertaken. Women found themselves excluded from the policy-making conferences

100

and relegated to the same clerical positions that they would have held in conservative organizations. The problem grew so obvious that SDS leader Tom Hayden spoke out: "The question (male chauvinism) cannot be postponed until 'after the revolution' because revolution is not possible without sharp personal breaks with bourgeois patterns of life, especially with America's repressive and property-oriented male and female relationships."

Despite statements such as this the achievement of female equality, purely through socialist revolution or evolution, remains problematic. Socialism and its proponents have a profound effect on the WL Movement both in the United States and in England. The chief reason for this is that the institutions of socialist realities such as 24-hour child-care centers, maternity leaves with guarantees of returns to the same jobs or their equivalents, and compensation for time taken off for parturition are necessary for the full equality of women.

The difficulty is that socialist theory would emancipate women in order to acquire a larger work force and not to aid in their self-actualization. Therefore full emancipation of women cannot occur under socialism. The classic socialist approach to the "Woman Question" has been summarized by H. Eckstein-Diener:

The thesis of Marx and Engels that economic production and the social form that it brings about make up the foundation for the political and intellectual history of every epoch forms the basis of the sociological approach to patriarchy and matriarchy. History, therefore, is not more than the story of class struggles between exploiters and exploited, dominated and dominating classes, at various levels of social development. The causes of all things are purely economical: religion, ethics, and art are only among the many facets of ideological superstructure . . . Matriarchy can only arise, if during an era, the woman determines the reproduction process and thus becomes the 'dominant class.' Sociology places this era at the only possible stage, the primitive agricultural level. Matriarchy would therefore be a transitional phenomenon, that brief period when the male is still a roaming hunter, while the woman has arrived at primitive agriculture.'"

Engels has reduced the problem of woman to her separation, from work and the means of production, by life in the family. As Juliet Mitchell has written: "The position of women, then, in the work of Marx and Engels remains dissociated from, or subsidiary to, a discussion of the family, which is in its turn subordinated merely as a precondition of private property. Their solutions retain this overly economist stress, or enter the realm of dislocated speculation."

Despite her radical criticism of the non-revolutionary conception of women in revolutionary analysis, Mitchell still finds that "Unlike her non-productive status, her capacity for maternity *is* a definition of woman." She is concerned to show throughout her essay that the liberation of woman must be achieved through socialism. This is rather like the psychiatrists who insist that Freudian theories of women are valid—if you delete the misognyistic passages. Mitchell cannot make the break with the male intellectualizations that rule radical socialism.

What feminism needs is not a reworking of Marx and Engels or a re-evaluation of Freud but a whole new thought of its own: based on a feminine history of culture and a feminine orientation of the social order and psychological experience. This is the only way that women can discover themselves.

Juliet Mitchell reconciles the fact of women's oppression with the venerated male ideologies but only by defining women as insurmountably subordinate to men because of their biology. This is what socialist doctrine has to offer to women. When women look to anthropological findings rather than to male theorizations of history, they can prove that maternity is *not* the invariable determinant of the social subordination of women.

It is possible to reject the entire male ideological superstructure. As Bachofen pointed out: "The mother's connection with the child is accessible unto sense perception and remains always a natural truth. But the father as begetter presents an entirely different character. Standing in no visible relation to the child, he can never, even in the marital relationship, cast off a certain fictive character. Belonging to the offspring only through the mediation of the mother, he always appears as the remoter potency."[2]

Among the Kamchatkans, the people inhabiting the peninsula between northeastern Soviet Russia and Asia, "The men do not like to leave home and children, even for a few hours." Kamchatkan women monopolize public affairs and all property of value. Domestic work is considered beneath their dignity. It is the man's duty.

"The Encounter Bay Tribe" (a South Australian people) "believe that paternal care is indispensable, for which reason women prefer to kill immediately any babies born after their fathers' death."[3]

As Eckstein-Diener has correlated, "The prevailing sex always secures freedom and dominion by supporting the dominated sex." This is achieved by assigning the passive role in the house to the other, while giving itself the most important and decisive affairs outside the house. Marxist and socialist, please note that the prevailing sex may be female or male despite the correlation of females with maternity.

Socialism postulates that dominion is invariably associated with the control of the means of production and that the means of production shape mental processes to a predictable pattern. Socialism determines that capitalism is the ultimate oppressor of women despite recorded anthropological findings that "matriarchy is possible at all cultural levels, disregarding the question of who owns or controls the means of production."[4]

The contradictions presented above notwithstanding, the determination that it is capitalism, and not cultural, psychological and traditionalized patterns of men that oppress women, is one of the two major bases for attacking women's oppression. A Marxist such as Caroline Lund writes on the WL Movement in England purely as an extension of socialist struggle. She quotes one Englishwoman on the Women's Liberation Workshop: "They are led by Maoists, so have an anti-capitalist orientation, but generally consider themselves feminists." Lund's concluding observation is in the classic socialist tradition of liberating women in order to achieve a Greater Purpose. "We are now seeing the beginning of a new upsurge of feminism among women in Great Britain that certainly has great potential for aiding the general struggle against capitalism."[5] It is only fair to add that wage discrimination against women in Great Britain is very much more severe than in the U.S.A., and that this has given English feminism a class-struggle analysis.

Reactions to the socialist position on women vary. A radical feminist such as Beverly Jones effectively criticizes the SDS position on women's oppression by comparing the SDS Women's Manifesto in logic and vocabulary to a NAACP Urban League list of grievances and demands. She underlines the untenable position of feminists within the socialist movement in the following quote: "It must have been disappointing indeed to the women, who drew up the 'analysis of women's role' and insisted it be printed verbatim in New Left Notes, to find Castro quoted the following month in the *National Guardian* to the effect that he is assuredly grateful to the women of Cuba for having fought in the hills and otherwise aided the revolution, but now all that is past and women's place is once again servant to husband and children, in the home."

A Marxist such as Evelyn Reed believes that women from all social strata can work on certain issues (birth control and abortion on demand), but she is still Marxist enough to find the basic cause of women's oppression to be the class structure of our society. "On all fundamental questions concerning private property-holding, wealthy women are just as likely to uphold the status quo and their privileged positions as are wealthy men. Thus class against class must be the guiding line in the struggle for human liberation in general and women's liberation in particular. . . . This assertion of Marxist theory has been confirmed by the experience of all the victorious revolutions over the past century—from Russia to China and Cuba."[8]

I have already discussed the Cuban retreat on the issue of women's equality. After the revolution, Soviet Russia experimented briefly with full equality for women but soon reversed these attempts and denounced the single standard in sex—free love—as a bourgeois invention and bad for the State. Submission of women to home and family was reinstitutionalized but this time with the addition of women's obligation to work.

In China, women's oppression is lessened by bringing women into full-scale participation in agricultural and industrial life. Chinese women's liberation is mostly confined, however, to their economic life and the right to birth control and abortion on demand. Both are good for the State. In all other areas of existence, women are as oppressed as in other countries. In China there is no concept of self-actualization for women or men.

Marxist Evelyn Reed considers it "imperative for women to work out an effective theory and program which corresponds to their needs and can realize their objectives." She criticizes NOW for failing to name the class forces that prevent equality for women and for not "naming the methods of struggle that are required to win these demands."[9] Actually NOW's political platform is among the most highly specific and articulate in the movement. Radical feminists criticize NOW for its goals—power and position—not for its lack of program.

Reed generally seeks to discredit contemporary feminists with the epithet man-hating. The only WL group she praises is Boston's BREAD AND ROSES, many collectives of which are still very heavily socialist in their priorities.

Socialism, or historical materialism, views all political and social problems as economically based on the class monopoly of production and the unequal distribution of goods. As this analysis does not apply to the oppression of women, and as the implementation of socialism as it now exists oppresses women, socialism can not be considered a viable politic equalizing the position of women. However, some socialist institutions are necessary for women's liberation, as I have previously stated.

The eradication of women's oppression requires a single-minded concentration on the issues that determine the lives of women. Events of the twentieth century and of the early feminist movement have shown that where the oppression of women is not viewed as a singular intolerance—the oldest in human history—liberation of women will always be seen as an issue to be tied in with whatever radical socialist question is under review. Women demonstrators in such contexts will continue to be seen as ladies' auxiliaries organized in support of the correct issue.

The Women's Liberation Movement is almost entirely white and its members range in age from the teen years to the middle years. The bottom age-range is lowering all the time as high school students pick up the demand for a deciding voice in the determination of policies and practices in their schools.

There are few non-Caucasian women of any race. For example, New York's large Puerto Rican population has few if any members in the WL Movement.

Women of the minority races have not been offered substantial benefits by the movement's platform, which is tailored to the needs of its white, middle- and upper-middle-class membership. There are WL groups on every level of education from high school through graduate, medical, law and business schools. There is no on-going effort to reach ghetto women: partially because minority women are proud and jealous of their new ethnic power; partially because white women fear minority women and feminists grew up in the same climate of opinion that nourished the rest of racist America.

WL began among middle-class working wives and radical students. The agitation for occupational equality arose with the return to work of the suburban housewife. Once these women re-entered the business world they discovered a new identity—the oppressed working class. Women found themselves the last hired, last promoted and first fired.

The Women's Liberation Movement is a catch-all phrase that is currently used by a diversity of groups. There are women who are radicals but who are not primarily committed to women's issues. There are also within the WL those groups that are solely concerned with women's issues, but which do not undertake radical analysis of our society or active political work. REDSTOCKINGS is the group I discussed as an example of this politic.

Radical feminists believe that feminism is the only truly radical political cause now in existence. They have a strong case for this belief. To achieve the elimination of dominance in human relationships, sex roles, i.e., stereotyped male and female identities, would have to be eradicated. Our economy would have to extend so that everybody—women, minority groups, homosexuals, and all religions and castes—could have equal opportunities to be hired and advanced. Hierarchical systems would have to wither away. Radical feminists would replace them with systems in industry, government, the home and the military in which decision-making power would be widely diffused. Radical feminists advocate only those systems in which everyone has equal rights. They would sharply reduce the gaps between the most and least powerful groups in society. Radical feminists advocate social, economical, political, psychological (role-playing) experimentation: They wish us to invent a future in which it is possible for each individual to be self-regulating while striving to activate all personal capacities. The restrictions would be that no one could trespass on the freedom of others.

Throughout this book, I have used the terms Women's Liberation Movement and feminism interchangeably. I took this freedom even though there are women radicals within the WL Movement who are not ready to be called feminists. Increasingly, there is a shift within WL from primary identification with the New Left to unabashed espousal of top priority for women's rights. Furthermore, references to the WL Movement as the new feminism are steadily receiving more acceptance. This book is being written in the midst of this shift in attitudes and reflects, in its categories, definitions and vocabulary, the contemporaneous existence of different self-images in the movement for women's rights.

Consciousness-Raising

Consciousness-raising has proved to be the most widely practiced method in WL for the pragmatic association of disparate personalities and philosophies within small groups. Consciousness-raising is the greatly improved descendant of the T-groups that industrial psychologists instituted to effect a working team out of a group of men in competition for promotion. As Jane Howard has written, the "basic technique was first developed 21 years ago at the National Training Laboratories, a private organization that teaches people how to interrelate."[8] Supermarket executives, stewardesses, professionals, policemen and clerics are among their clients.

In the original T-groups, the personal problems of the men were seen as obstacles to be eradicated. Consciousness-raising in the WL Movement focuses on common, i.e., social, problems as the central issues to which political attention should be directed. T-group training was initiated to insure greater effectiveness on the job—much like the coffee break and one-hour lunch break. It was and is a means of socializing the employee.

Peace Corps Training constitutes a less obvious form of social coercion. Apparently an open-ended process, its ultimate goal is group conformity to government standards. As Peter Friedland, a former volunteer from the Peace Corps in the Philippines wrote:

The sickest thing about that atmosphere, and the feature most markedly right out of the coming totalitarian age, is how much of a threat the trainees are to each other; how easy it is to get them to accept and actively get involved in 'evaluating' each other for conditions of which they have no conception.

As Kitsi Burkhart said in her article for the Philadelphia *Bulletin*: "What pretended to be a healthy normality of people acting amiably toward each other was, in fact, pressure to conform—a muting of natural exuberance, intelligence and aggressiveness."

The purpose of such training sessions is to select out the highly personal ingredients that impede group goals and to fit the participants for undertaking their tasks. Consciousness-raising as practiced by feminists is the close examination of the individual lives of group members to determine how society must be changed to eliminate the oppression to which all women can testify.

Consciousness-raising techniques are part of the return of spirituality to America. They have many parallels in the Human Potential Movement, whose purpose is to unlock people's potential, but the Human Potential Movement and the Esalen Institute are apolitical. At the Esalen Institute on Big Sur, five-day series of encounter-group meetings "focus the attention of group members exclusively on their 'Here-and-Now' feelings about each other."

Dr. Abraham Maslow, an important spokesman for the Human Potential Movement, speaks of developing personalities capable of "peak experiences," and of "taking religion back from the priests."

In this sense religion and spiritualism can be among the most conservative of forces: leading to individual solutions or private joy despite social ills. The late Dr. Frederich Perls, founder of Gestalt therapy, says that the goal of the encounter technique is to integrate fragmented and seemingly unrelated aspects of the personality. The goal of consciousness-raising is to relate fragmented and seemingly unrelated problems in the lives of individual women and to construct a politic from the issues discovered in the process.

While consciousness-raising is widely practiced throughout the WL Movement, there are formal distinctions to be made in the way that different groups regard consciousness-raising and in the ways that they practice it. Most rap groups fall apart in a few months. Usually the group's membership is heterogeneous, and there is no common link binding the women together. Worst of all for the endurance of the group there is no analysis of the emotional experiences under discussion.

Probably REDSTOCKINGS has the most developed formulation of consciousness-raising. An examination of the group's goals and its failures may serve as an example of the dynamic as it is currently operating in the WL Movement. REDSTOCKINGS declares that consciousness-raising is not an end in itself but a means of acquiring information from which generalizations about the socialization of women can be made. Once the objective conditions of women's lives are identified the goal is analysis of possible methods of struggle against oppression and the growth of actions implementing these methods.

This is the ideal; the ways in which consciousness-raising has failed for REDSTOCKINGS, and can fail in other groups, has been excellently described by Jeanne Arrow of the FEMINISTS in her paper: *Dangers in the Pro-Women Line and Consciousness-raising.*

At first talking about yourself and sharing the similarity of other women's experiences is illuminating and encouraging. But months of speaking minutely about one's life and feelings defeats the original thrust towards objective truth and ends in increased subjectivity, mere self-indulgence, an ego trip on which to cover the ground of one's uniqueness again and again. It is also interesting that people generally enjoy talking about their past rather than present difficulties. . . . Consciousness-raising breeds a lot of clever insights but it never seeks to discover what is unique and what common among women, the distinctions between the essential institutions of our oppression and those that are secondary and incidental, that is the necessary method of attack, and what kind of structure would work for us in the future. There is no natural point at which consciousness-raising as the sole method of a group stops and work on theory begins. . . . The length of time spent on this one aspect of revolution is so extended that some women know nothing else about feminism after months in the movement.

The FEMINISTS are not the only group aware of the dangers of uncontrolled consciousness-raising. When the Stanton-Anthony Brigade wrote the Organizing Principles of the NEW YORK RADICAL FEMINISTS, the group stipulated that new groups wishing to join NYRF must complete a minimum of three months of consciousness-raising "in which you will talk about personal experience without broad analysis." The intention was that the new groups conclude these untheoretical sessions within the three-month period. NYRF see consciousness-raising as a means of building group intimacy and internal democracy, and of redirecting the group's anger to the institutions of oppression and of creating an understanding of the nature of politics. Consciousness-raising reveals the extension of institutional and socio-economic oppression into the most private spheres of every woman's being.

The NYRF's conception of consciousness-raising is to be distinguished from the FEMINISTS'. The FEMINISTS would use consciousness-raising as an "organizing tool alone." They don't believe that relationships that develop within feminist groups must be constantly open to analysis just because subjective experiences and interpersonal relationships are the stuff of politics. Once the group's commitment to formulated goals has been secured through the "organizing tool" of consciousness-raising, the FEMINISTS seem to believe that further expression of subjective experiences becomes a danger to revolutionary action. Actually other radical feminists have come to the realization that theory must come from constant examination of personal experiences. Political theory must be derived from life. Politics is *not* something decided in the head and then followed willy-nilly whatever the changes in personal experience.

Some groups have confined themselves to consciousness-raising without actions or political analysis and managed to endure as political entities. They have accomplished this by confining their sessions to their experiences in the here-and-now. Such groups act to support each other in their attempts at self-definition, and liberate each member's energy as they increase her self-confidence. In one particular group even though the group itself did not undertake political actions or develop a political theory, its members became active organizing and radicalizing people on their jobs and in their communities.

Consciousness-raising on this level, as a purely supportive experience that constantly considers the aspirations, cultural conditioning and options open to the women in a group, can perform the function in female education recently outlined by Pauline Tompkins, president of Cedar Crest College. Dr. Tompkins asserted that women frequently underestimate their intellectual, social and personal competencies and women's education must redress this inequity in the socialization of women and men.

Feminists approve Valerie Solanis's work as a brilliant piece of consciousness-raising. The Solanis SCUM (Society to Cut Up Men) Manifesto is not viewed as a schema for political action but as a poetic leap of the imagination forcing new insights into the roles that women and men play. It reverses the perspective of the man-woman relationship. Man is no longer the predator but the vulnerable one. The SCUM Manifesto reveals the nature of sexism more clearly than it has ever been shown before.

Radical socialists reject consciousness-raising as a revolutionary activity. To purists, consciousness-raising, which they see as inseparable from the pro-woman line, is based in the liberal bourgeoisie. Karen Frankel writes:

At the heart of the support for such middle-class movements is a very primitive anti-Marxist conception of how to raise people's consciousness. The SWP, IS RYM II, etc view the raising of consciousness in a totally idealist and subjective manner. The question of abortion reform" (actually the WLM advocates repeal, *not* reform) "is a perfect example. They hold to the opinion that a woman's consciousness is raised . . . by her beginning to understand that she can control her own body. . . . This is a far cry from Trotsky's conception of raising consciousness as outlined in the Transitional Program. It poses nothing in class terms and bows completely to middle class subjectivity. The problem is the understanding of the need to control society, not your own body. To start with the need to control your own body is to start subjectively, and to start subjectively is to end subjectively. The middle class can never get very far from subjectivity. (Actually it is the subjective realization that self-definition could only be attained in a society that had been changed to allow great freedom of self-manifestation that radicalized American youth in the 60's).

Furthermore such a conception raises false consciousness. . . . Even with abortion law repeal, they still live under capitalism and have to sell their bodies every day on the job market.

The demand for day-care centers, in and of themselves or even in combination with abortion reform, does not constitute the raising of socialist consciousness. People do not come to socialist consciousness by revolutionists propagandizing to them about how they have to control their own bodies, but by the day in and day out struggles led by revolutionaries against the bosses to build a decent life for themselves and their children.[9]

Many of the problems that arise in women's liberation groups are by no means peculiar to the feminist movement. WLM is a movement of small groups and their problems are the problems of the small-group dynamic familiar to every unionist, women's club member, fraternity-man and workshop participant. In short, this analysis must be familiar to every reader of small-group psychology. The divisions that arise within the groups are class background differences, racial differences, marital status differences. Every group develops a continual argument between its reformers and its revolutionaries.

One constant source of conflict is the fear that some feminists have that the movement is only being used by women as a proving grounds for the development of their skills which they will then sell to the male-dominated world. WLM has given many women their first opportunities to work independently on projects or to develop authority. In mixed groups women are rarely allowed to exercise any competence or learn any administrative strategy.

Still this fear of betrayal, which is sure to be well-founded in some cases, may possibly lead to the very stunting of individual ability that WLM was formed to combat. One fears the possibility of repression such as that met by John Garfield when he was a member of Group Theater. According to Richard Schickel, when John Garfield was offered a film contract: "That rather self-righteous collection of actors actually held a meeting to register their disapproval of Garfield's trip to Hollywood. Among his grievances was the Group's absurd failure to cast him as Golden Boy, relegating him to a minor part where he could watch the miscast Luther Adler do a part for which Garfield was born. The Group may have polished Garfield's talent, but its lingering effect on him was to create doubts about the value of his work, the reality of his talent."[10]

The goal of the WLM should be for every woman to be all of herself in each moment; in the words of Carl Rogers, "all the richness and complexity, with nothing hidden from oneself, and nothing feared in oneself " Woman have had to fear self-actualization for so long that now is the time to welcome the chance for complete selfhood.

One of the reasons for the tension in the movement about women coming infrequently to meetings or dropping in and out of groups is the spectre of the group's dissolution. In this context, failures to attend meetings or participate in demonstrations may be viewed as a lessening of enthusiasm for feminist causes. This is particularly frightening to a very young movement. Feminist groups that have been 100% committed to women's issues from their inception generally have more difficulty developing beyond the initial joy of discovering the allegiance and sisterhood of all women as oppressed people. As the group's members gradually acquire organizational expertise and gain confidence in their own commitment, these fears are greatly diminished.

The evolution, then, within autonomous feminist groups, is generally from the joy of recognition of a common oppression, to a repressive attitude to any commitment to people and activities outside the group, to a realization that the strength of the group lies in the fulfillment of its members in every area of their lives—both in and out of the group.

Women's liberation groups that start out as caucuses that have seceded from male-dominated groups have a somewhat different evolution. These women already are familiar with political procedure and processes. Their groups are at first more cohesive than the autonomous feminist groups because of the initial advantage of their political association with male groups.

The disadvantages of their past associations are many. Ex-"Movement" women often experience guilt about focusing on women's issues as they have difficulty believing that women's oppression is a valid political issue. Much time is spent in nostalgic attempts at re-creating facsimiles of the organizations that they have just left. Such women insist on acting in coalition with any demonstration called by the New Left. Perhaps what they miss most of all is the discipline of an established "correct" analysis. The absence of strong authority and the accompanying uncertainties and divisions of a newly reborn movement whose political terms and philosophical bases have yet to be defined are understandably frightening. For example, women

116

radicals will generally refer to themselves as "very heavy into women's lib" rather than identify themselves as feminists. After all, these women have been nurtured on the same mythologies that inhabit the consciousness of every American: the self-confidence, aggression and arrogance of "The Street-Fighting Man" that we have all been taught to desire whether they appear in Robert F Kennedy or Mick Jagger.

Eventually women radicals seem to realize that they have re-incarnated the male gestalt in their collectives, and they are faced with the same uncertainties and fears as the other women in the movement. The common problem is the difficulty of creating authentically female myths and orientations.

One of the greatest impediments to full equality for women is their fear of being ostracized and of losing their feminine qualities if they assert themselves. Women reason that if they are not "women," that is, beings defined by their relation to men, they are nothing. Fear of the radical extension of the self to achieve an unknown identity is one of the major inhibitions that feminism must overcome. Feminism is the most radical political and social doctrine in the history of our civilization just because it advocates being as a process without rigid definitions.

There is a tendency that WLM shares with other groups of speaking only to one's own—not bothering to develop the vocabulary and the insight that allow dialectic with people of different persuasions. There is a tendency all too common in any movement to belittle and even exaggerate the differences that separate the various groups. Impatient irritability was the very frequent response in the first years of the movement to the suggestion that new people be allowed in the group. The I've-gone-through-all-those-changes-and-I-can't-retrace-all-that-time reaction was a constant source of dissension. Whether this reaction is grounded in elitism is arguable, but the problem of admitting new mem-

117

bers to a smoothly functioning group is only just beginning to be solved.

When new women come into a feminist group, they often have little knowledge of feminism, have not begun to identify the causes of their oppression and sometimes do not even know what they want from the movement. To educate each new member or influx of new members means going back over ideas and discussions already familiar to the older members. This is tedious and prevents the group from making any progress in political analysis or planning actions.

Also once a group has been fuctioning for a period of several months, each of the members has assumed a symbiotic relationship to the whole. The women trust each other and their ability to be candid is threatened by the appearance of new women whose attitudes and politics are unknown. The problem of personality preferences and common assumptions enters here as well. A group may not want to deal with women whose ideas and mores are greatly at variance with theirs and who strongly contest the group's program. Often these disruptive ideas are problems that the group feels it has already solved.

Just as frequently it is the new member's style and personality or her naivete that annoys the group. Women want to be in a group all of whose members are bright, knowledgeable and interesting. This natural concomitant of the intimacies of consciousness-raising can also lead to elitism: the feeling that the group is very well just as it is. This of course is contrary to the political aims of the WLM, which are to build a mass movement that will be able to effect radical change in our society.

Many groups are closed to new members so that interested women may experience some difficulty in finding a group that will admit them. Still, there are valid reasons for closing a group. It is often necessary to keep the membership to the size within which close feeling and collective thinking can be maintained. Fifteen is generally considered the maximum number feasible for full participation in consciousness-raising.

The Women's Liberation Movement and the Great Society

Feminists contend that the oppression of women begins in the family. Little girls are given dolls to play with, bigger girls are taught to support the male ego. Educational institutions continue this channeling of women into dependent roles. Feminists believe that there can be no real equality in our society until relationships between the sexes are restructured. The inegalitarian relations within the home are seen as the basis of all evil.

Feminists recognize that any social reconstruction must consider the affectional needs of both women and men. Most feminists see all-female communes as tentative experiments with new domestic arrangements, not as ultimate solutions for the human need for love and a spiritual home. Feminists hope to design new living arrangements "which will make our co-existence with men in the future all the more equal and the more humane."

Some extreme groups of feminists wish to abolish relationships with men and wifehood and motherhood as roles uniquely oppressive. It is not clear whether those who advocate this separation of the sexes intend it as a transitory phase until the sexes can reorder social roles and eliminate domination from human relationships, or if they intend the definite termination of relationships with half the people in the world, i.e., men.

Dr. Jessie Bernard recently told a World Future Society audience that the WLM is "preparing us for a world in which men and women are going to relate to one another in ways quite removed from reproduction.

119

"These radical women are helping us catch up with revolutions which have already occurred or are in process . . ." They "represent an avant garde that is going to enormously modify all our projections.

"They are, in brief, anticipating a future in which loving and affectionate companionship between the sexes will be possible based on mutual recognition of one another as individuated human beings rather than as stereotypical male and female beings."

Speaking for feminists, she addressed the men in the audience: "You can devote yourself to your work wholeheartedly because you have a servant at home who takes care of the dull chores of homemaking. You are not accustomed to doing monotonous, repetitive work which never results in any lasting, let alone important, achievement."

Most feminists intend to keep relating to men, but they realize that no man is free of prejudice toward women and that they cannot hope to convince men as a group to relinquish their privileges simply through intellectual or moral arguments. In our society, the male's need to dominate the female is deeply rooted in his psyche and our institutions. Sexism, the belief that men are more important than women because they are better than them, is not a phenomenon between two individuals in a relationship. It is a social attitude that pervades every element in our civilization. Only by organizing and supporting each other can women effect the social changes necessary for full equality between women and men.

Analysis of the man's problem is necessary for women to develop good consciousness, but action is another problem. . . .The disease is social and must be dealt with politically. We cannot 'work out' the problem with a man or men, any more than we can transfer the problem to an all-female situation. That would mean simply finding comfort there and returning to our cages. Homosex-

120

uality is again no more than a personal 'solution'. . . . Our attitude should lead up to separation from men who are not consciously working for female liberation, not sectarianism in an all-female movement. . . . Hatred and resentment of men are not sufficient to give women lasting energy to fight. . . . Recognition of the SOCIAL nature of the oppression of women is our first step to consciousness.[11]

NOW differs from radical feminism because it does not wish to abolish power. NOW's goals are in the classic tradition of political parties in our society. Like most political groups, it wishes to shift the power from those who have it to those who don't: from men to women. NOW "wants to get women into positions of power."

Feminist time is not like standard time in America. Liaisons are formed, educations are acquired, philosophies are discarded, and groups form, reconstitute themselves and dissolve all in a matter of seasons. Feminists move from city to city, often to meet other women known from their last location. And all the time there is the excitement of knowing that women are making history. The time has come. . . .

Abortion

Presently, abortion is the one issue on which all women's groups have agreed to fight. Establishing child-care centers is the only other issue that comes close to winning universal support. In fact, this is so very true that some women have been uneasy lest contemporary feminism coagulate into the mortal shape of the earlier movement. Nineteenth-century feminism became a one-issue politics and died when that for which it struggled—suffrage—was attained.

Resistance to changes in abortion lessened dramatically in 1967, when feminism declared itself a movement. That year California and Colorado included new grounds for legal abortion in their state laws. In California, the Therapeutic Abortion Act legalized abortion in cases where pregnancies are caused by rape or incest and when pregnancies threaten the physical and mental health of the mother. Formerly abortion was permitted only to save the mother's life. Colorado and the eight other states that have liberalized their laws have legalized abortion as well when there is a likelihood that a child will be born deformed. However, according to the *National Observer,* in 1969, "a total of 35 states considered drastic revisions of abortion limits . . . and rejected the idea."

In those ten states where the abortion laws have been liberalized, there has been no considerable alleviation of the problem of compulsory pregnancy. In Colorado and California the laws have been found to benefit only those women with the money and education to fulfill all the qualifications for strict eligibility. (The women enabled to have abortions by the reformed laws are almost entirely white and of the middle and upper classes.)

Discontent with these results have brought liberals, radicals and feminists to discard the goal of abortion law reform and to fight instead for repeal of all such laws. The character and form of the opposition has also changed. Previously opponents tried to change abortion laws through legislative means in the representative assemblies of their states; now their attack is focused on litigation to prove the unconstitutionality of abortion laws and the invidious discriminations inherent in the liberalized laws.

This effort at settling the matter in the courts has eased the pressure on the legislators; many representatives would prefer a complete repeal of all abortion laws to the responsibility of determining at which point termination of a pregnancy becomes murder.

In a recent decision that is presently being appealed

to the Supreme Court, Federal District Judge Gerhard A. Gesell held that the Washington, D.C., abortion law was unconstitutionally vague and was probably an unconstitutional infringement upon women's private rights.

Judge Gesell said there has been "an increasing indication in decisions of the Supreme Court of the United States that as a secular matter, a woman's liberty and right of privacy extends to family, marriage and sex matters, and may well include the right to remove an unwanted child, at least in the early stages of pregnancy." Judge Gesell said that the present D.C. law put the physician in a "particularly unconscionable position because it didn't take into consideration the mental and emotional health of the mother." The judge further contended that the statute was unconstitutional because it placed on the physician the burden of proving that the operation was necessary to save the mother's life.

In New York there are four Federal court suits challenging the constitutionality of the state abortion law. The American Civil Liberties Union filed a suit on behalf of four doctors declaring that the laws restricted their freedom to practice medicine.

The other suit that has received considerable press coverage is that filed by the Law Commune, a group active in social causes on behalf of 125 physicians, lawyers, social workers, psychologists and writers, almost all of whom are women. All 125 people are plaintiffs in the suit and the Women's Liberation Movement has been demonstrating and seeking out other women to appear as plaintiffs and sign petitions for repeal of the law. There are more than 300 plaintiffs involved in the several suits pending in New York. These women then testified as to their experiences, professional or personal, with abortions. Their testimony is part of a deposition that was turned over to the three-judge Federal Court hearing the combined suits challenging the law. REDSTOCKINGS' protest, that abortion law reform was being undertaken without the consent and advice of women, would appear to have altered the procedures in handling the most personal of women's issues.

The suit was submitted by four women attorneys. Marcia Lowry told *The New York Times,* "On paper, we're all being very moral, but in fact, we all know that it is the poor women who have to pay. They don't have a permanent relationship with a family doctor; they can't express themselves well; they can't afford to get certified by psychiatrists. There has to be something wrong with a law that makes legal abortion so much more available to white women. Even if the law doesn't have that intent, it certainly has that effect." Her suit claims that this is a violation of equal protection under the law.

"Our job is to convince the judges of something that is as plain to me as day—that every woman has the right to bring this suit, that these laws affect every woman's sex life whether she is pregnant or not. It can't be more obvious that this is one law that has been incredibly oppressive of women and has seriously hurt many, many women,"[12] said Nancy Stearns, staff lawyer with Arthur Kinoy's Law Center for Constitutional Rights. Florynce R. Kennedy, a woman lawyer active in radical causes ranging from the Black Panthers to feminism, says that actions might be brought in the names of unborn children who might not wish to be born unless guaranteed comfortable circumstances.

One of the most effective battles against abortion statutes is being waged in Massachusetts. The suit challenges the state's right to make moral judgments about private affairs and contends that the anti-abortion law is merely a legislative extension of the beliefs of the Roman Catholic Church. The suit in Massachusetts revolves around the case of a doctor accused of violating the state's abortion law. His lawyer contends that the indictment should be dropped because the abortion statute is constitutionally invalid because: "It establishes a religious position, particularly the Roman Catholic Church's position, against allowing abortions

. . . to the exclusion of the positions of other religions
. . . nonreligious groups, and persons." Massachusetts,
Louisiana, New Jersey and Pennsylvania are the only
states in America that have not enacted some liberali-
zation of the general prohibition against abortion.

The countrywide change in attitudes toward abortion
exploded into the public consciousness last September
when the California Supreme Court ruled that the
state's abortion statute was unconstitutional. The abortion statutes of more than 35 other states are vulnerable to the attack that won the case in California. The
law may be claimed to be unconstitutionally vague and
a denial of fundamental rights to women and their doctors.

The Women's Liberation Movement is not the only
group supporting abortion law repeal. Some others are:

> Physicians' Forum
> Federation of Protestant Welfare Agencies, New
> York City
> American Public Health Association, Governing
> Council
> Planned Parenthood-World Population, Medical
> Committee
> Unitarian-Universalist Association
> American Jewish Congress
> Menninger Foundation, Dept. of Preventive Psy-
> chiatry
> Medical Committee for Human Rights
> Citizens' Advisory Council on the Status of
> Women, 1968
> Local 1199, Drug and Hospital Employees
> Union, New York City
> American Ethical Union
> Social Service Employees Union, New York City
> Americans for Democratic Action
> American Humanist Association
> National Emergency Civil Liberties Committee

The latest Gallup Poll showed 40% of the nation's adults favor legislation permitting women to terminate pregnancy during the first three months. Hawaii has just become the first state in the Union to agree to abortion on request for any woman over 20. This statute leaves the decision to abort in the realm of medical advice and individual will.

Jane E. Brody wrote recently in *The New York Times* that there are growing signs of substantive increase in support for repeal of abortion laws. At least 13 state legislatures are now considering bills such as Hawaii's that convert abortion from a crime to a purely medical matter between doctors and their patients and that demand no medical prerequisites before doctors can legally perform abortions. Jane Brody wrote that "the current emphasis on repeal of abortion laws is a direct outgrowth of what many abortion law activists regard as an unsuccessful experiment with" abortion law reform. The reform laws have not benefited the vast majority of women seeking abortions and they have also come under strong criticism from the Roman Catholic Church. To Catholics repeal is a lesser evil than reform because it takes the state out of the position of deciding who shall or shall not be born.

An editorial in *The New York Times* refers to the change in public attitudes on abortion as revolutionary while others feel that the current upsurge of debate on abortion is a rather dramatic evolution in public attitudes.

The changes brought about through court decisions reflect dissent but do not reflect broad-scale radical changes in public opinion as the same changes would if made through the legislature.

Three main characteristics of today's abortion repeal movement are: 1) demanding repeal rather than reform; 2) using litigation rather than legislation to get it; 3) taking the view that abortion on demand is a fundamental right of women of all classes and all races.

Abortion reform laws discriminate in favor of the

rich and educated. Roy Lucas, a lawyer contesting the constitutionality of New York's law, has stated that "90 percent of the women who get legal abortions are white, while about 90 percent of those who die from illegal ones are black or Puerto Rican."[13] The New York suit also argues that the state's abortion statute subverts the provisions of the Bill of Rights that create the right to marital and sexual privacy.

The struggle to repeal abortion laws has representative organizations throughout America. There is the NARAL (The National Association for Abortion Repeal) and many states have a counterpart, NYALR (New Yorkers for Abortion Law Repeal). Instructions for women wishing to campaign are:

1. "Write your own state legislators and your governor to tell them you are for REPEAL. Urge them to introduce a bill in the state legislature or to co-sponsor a repeal bill that has been introduced.

2. "Talk with or write to friends around the state that you think would be sympathetic to repeal; encourage them to write their legislators.

3. "Ask your doctor to urge his legislators to support repeal; ask him to join with his colleagues in working to abolish the hospital 'abortion committees' that hamper their freedom to provide good medical care. Hospital abortion committees are so restrictive that even in cases where abortion can be legally performed, formal approval often comes too late for safe abortion.

4. "If you are a member of a church, union, political group, professional organization, or any other organization, urge the group to take a public stand for repeal —and only REPEAL. Encourage the members to support this stand by working actively for repeal."

NOW and NYALR have put out an Abortion Counseling Information sheet that has been revised as of February, 1970. The sheet warns under general comments that women should be certain that they are pregnant before seeking help from a counseling service. Women are also asked to "avoid using the word abortion" in phone conversation with the services or with the doctors. When they refer you to someone, say you "have a problem" or something similar. Women are urged to comparison shop both quality of services and doctors.

Listed are the *Abortion Counseling Service* ACS P.O. Box 9199, San Diego, Calif. 92109 (714) 233-4514. "Run by a group of young women only for San Diego County Residents. Arranges for discreet pregnancy tests and consultations with sympathetic physicians. ACS has an excellent newsletter that could serve as a model for other groups just beginning. $2.00 to be on the newsletter mailing list."

Association to Repeal Abortion Laws (ARAL) P.O. Box 6083, San Francisco, Calif. 94101 (415) 387-6480. "For a $5.00 donation to ARAL they will send you very detailed advice and a list of abortion specialists—mostly in Mexico, but also in Puerto Rico and Japan that ARAL keeps close tabs on; the list is updated constantly for your safety, and should *always* be freshly purchased. Help available through 7 months."

Clergy Consultation Service (On Abortion/on Problem Pregnancies, etc.) "These services are located in several cities and are run by groups of ministers and rabbis. Each service generally counsels with women from its state or area only. Clergy services will soon be in open operation in Montreal and other cities. To find out if there is someone already available in your area for counseling write the National Clergy Consultation Service on Abortion, 55 Washington Square South, NYC 10012, or call weekdays between 9 A.M. and noon Eastern Standard Time (212) 254-6314. These services have received some foundation support for their work. Most of them maintain tape-recorded messages at the numbers given below which announce that five or six ministers and rabbis are available for counseling that week, and give instructions on procedures to follow in setting up an appointment with the one you choose. They will instruct you to bring with you a dated note signed by an obstetrician/gynecologist who has examined you internally, saying how many weeks pregnant you are. Be sure to get this note before calling them. The CCS uses out-of-state doctors and foreign doctors (Puerto Rico, England, Japan) and provides help up to 22 weeks. Those over 12 weeks are referred to England."

California (Los Angeles)
  (213) 666-7600
Connecticut (New Haven)
  (203) 624-8646
Illinois (Chicago)
  (312) 667-6015
Iowa
  (515) 282-1738
Massachusetts (Boston)
  (617) 527-7188
Michigan (Detroit)
  (313) 964-0838

New Jersey (northern)
  (201) 933-2937
New York City & suburbs
  (212) 477-0034*
New York State (Buffalo area)
  (716) 632-0441
New York State (Ithaca area)
  (607) 272-7172
Ohio (Cleveland)
  (216) 229-7423
Pennsylvania (Philadelphia)
  (215) 923-5141

       *no messages giving names from 5 P.M. Fri. to 10 A.M. Mon.

Parents' Aid Society, 130 Main Street, Hempstead, Long Island, New York 11550. (516) 538-2626 or 437-2828. "Be sure to place all telephone calls person-to-person to Bill Baird . . . founder and director of the Society. Parents' Aid gives advice on both local and distant sources of help, and tries to help any woman who comes to them; women visiting the clinic should try to bring the man involved if possible . . . Contraceptive advice and materials are also available."

Women's Assistance Tour, New York City (212) 245-2569. "This air tour to an eastern European city —that has excellent medical facilities and attitudes to match—is run by a woman. You must have 1) a doctor's note saying how many weeks pregnant you are (not over 12 weeks); 2) a record of a current vaccination; 3) a passport . . . You leave on a Wednesday night plane, are met at your destination, and are back home Sunday evening. The total cost is now $900, if you leave from the east coast (more from points west), but volume may soon bring the price down to a lower figure. This includes: air fare, lodging in first-class hotels, meals, in-city transportation, medical care, and post-abortion check-up, 24-hour English language information service and sightseeing!"[14]

The difficulty with all the services offered is that they require money and a degree of self-assurance and competence in arranging affairs that lower-class and minority women often do not have.

In the United States the maternal mortality rate, excluding deaths from abortion, is about 25 per 100,000 (there were 3,535,000 births here in 1969). Linda Greenhouse makes a useful comparison between death rates from abortion in countries where they are available on demand in hospitals and deaths from childbirth in hospitals: hospital abortion death rate—3 per 100,000; hospital childbirth death rate—25 per 100,000; It is tight times safer to have an abortion than have a baby.[15]

Anthropologists have noted that the most distinguishing characteristic of a matriarchy is the woman's free disposition over her own body (white feminists at the New Haven Black Panther demonstrations sang "My Body is Mine to Control"). She may prevent pregnancy or terminate it whenever she wishes.

Society's Reaction to the Movement or the Frontierman Meets the Liberated Woman

Few subjects arouse such emotional responses in men as women's rights. When a woman spoke to a mixed audience suggesting that in the future men would feel free to stay home and housekeep and mind the babies while their wives worked, male reaction in the audience exploded into childish language, vituperation

130

and the assertion that women were witches as bosses and impossible in intellectual confrontations. The men gnashed their teeth when she suggested that men enjoyed the freedom to create only because they have wives to keep their homes and lives in order.

As Roxanne Dunbar and Lisa Leghorn sapiently remarked, "No man plays a passive role in the oppression of females . . . Men not only support the caste system, they are terrified of losing any part of it. A bare rumbling from women is exaggerated to the scale of an army of castrating Amazons . . . His (the man's) only justification for existence lies in his *being a man*, which means possessing the right to oppress a woman (in the family) and feel superior to women in general. Any man who is not working consciously to change the inequal relationship of men and women is opposing the interests of women."[16]

As the WL Movement is publicized more and more, women increasingly run into such remarks from men as, "Those feminists scare the hell out of me!" or "The very thought of women's rights gives me a cold shiver." From women, they meet with a reaction not very different from that encountered by the early feminists when they urged women to petition for suffrage. Often those 19th-century housewives slammed the door in the petitioner's face saying that they didn't need the vote as *they* had husbands to care for them. Modern women hearing that friends of theirs have joined WL or a feminist group, frequently exclaim: but that's a bunch of maladjusted women. *You* don't want to have anything to do with them; or, *You've got a man, what are you doing with those manhaters?*

Judith Brown has analyzed the real fear behind some of the abuse that feminists meet with:

Indirect male sniping, insinuating homosexuality is a horror which is bound to attend female liberation activity, has some interesting analogies in our movement experience . . . Our answers to red-baiting will serve us well here. The charge of homosexuality—which will be openly voiced by non-movement males—stands for a fear of something greater, as did the charge of communism against southern blacks and whites getting together: that they might get together. An indigenous movement of any people determined to gain their liberation is a more serious threat than 'communism' or 'homosexuality' and the charge is merely a delaying tactic to obstruct organization."

The reactions of men generally liberal on other subjects are revelatory of the irrational nature of the resistance to women's equality. Pete Hamill, a New York journalist who supported Bernadette Devlin's fight for Irish socialism and who frequently writes about social injustices, took refuge in the full panoply of derisive remarks about women. In a column heavy with sarcasm, he warns, "Wait a minute: this women's liberation number is starting to get serious . . . Hombres, muchachos, defend yourselves: the termagants are coming and we must band together as brothers."

He denounces abortion reform saying "in the age of the pill, it is a rare or stupid girl who gets herself pregnant; if a girl shares pleasure, why should she not face the consequences?"

Familiarly enough he implies that full employment of women would be taking jobs away from black males and that if women want real equality they should join the armed services or demand the abolition of alimony. Many women would not join any army because of their moral opposition to war and violence. NOW and many feminists are working for the abolition of alimony right now. Mr. Hamill has not checked his facts.

It is significant of the depth of his dislike of women that he also brings up the subject that women are not as great creators, artists and rulers as men. He uses as his control period the thousands of years when women did not have access to education and the stimulation of public life.[18]

Very often criticisms of the Women's Liberation Movement ignore the facts. Margaret Mead criticizes feminists stating that their demands are too superficial to effect the necessary change in women's roles to meet the crisis of the population explosion. Dr. Mead's point is that in the future, because of overpopulation, people will have to be oriented to find self-fulfillment through other roles than parenthood. She completely ignores the fact that radical feminists are even now rejecting the necessity of the nuclear family and childbearing as the ultimate goal of womanhood. Women's liberation groups in general are even now experimenting with new ways of living together to achieve the warmth and satisfaction of family life without its limitations and without overpopulating our world.

There is indeed a "durable cultural fantasy that feminine assertiveness—political, professional or sexual —is but a symptom of raging nymphomania or other grave psychic disorders."[19]

The perfect example of this view of women's liberation as at best a liberation of women to enjoy unbridled sexual intercourse is the recent *Harper's Magazine* article by Edward Grossman. The cover of that particular issue showed a woman's thighs bare almost to the crotch—with a headline asking, *What do women want? My God, what do they want?* This article represents a backlash to the WL Movement. The climax of this piece is his admission of uneasiness at the thought of women seeking equality. However, his ultimate point was that women have greater sexual potentialities than men and their realization of this would be the main result of the new feminism. Mr. Grossman's theory is no more than a new variation on the theme of women as totally sexual creatures. According to Grossman liberation for women will mean only the right to enjoy as many orgasms as they desire with whomever they desire.

Another example of male backlash is the formation

133

of an all-male society that wishes to fight for the continuation of the male as head of the family. SEAM, Society for the Emancipation of the Male, is located in Ann Arbor, Michigan. The feminine counterpart to this is the Pussycats, a league of women who dislike feminists because they are not "real women." The Pussycats say, "Why, the poor querulous creatures. They're mostly obese and have skin problems. They're afraid they'll never get a man to love them. That's why they have razor blades sticking out of their elbows. And feminists they call themselves. They should call themselves masculinists. Heaven knows they try to look like men and act like men."[20]

It is the fear of just such remarks as the above that keeps many women from organizing for their rights. Women such as the Pussycats who prefer to accomplish their aims by manipulating men are furious with any women who would equalize our society and end the manipulation of one human being by another.

Columnist Harriet Van Horne also criticized the demonstrators at the Miss America Pageant as a "band of ferocious feminists afflicted with a virulent case of neurotic frustration." She described them as "those sturdy lasses in their sensible shoes," criticizing them for not being feminine and, thus, ignoring the feminists' argument that women should not be valued according to their appeal to men. Miss Van Horne finished off with "Most of us would rather be some dear man's boob girl than nobody's cum laude scholar."

In another article covering a Yale coeds' revolt against the administration's intended decrease in the number of women to be admitted to next year's freshman class, the reporter, sympathetic to the Yale women, thought it necessary to emphasize such details as their rooms being "dominated by feminine touches including flowers." Her first quote from the students is that they "don't believe in the women's lib movement." "I don't agree with their tactics." The girls' central complaint is that being the only girl in a class prevents natural reactions. "You're forced to play a role." Actually these girls are feminists but they are afraid of the criticism of such as Pete Hamill, Harriet Van Horne, and the Pussycat League. Obviously their role playing was advantageous.

They got a sympathetic press which is usually not the case when feminists are honest. The article ends with one roommate asking softly: "Do you have to be a male to be a leader?" The softness is the thing.

Consider the condescending tone of the following description of a women's liberation group. "They were all under 30, rather pleasant-looking housewives trying to look like radicals by not wearing makeup and not shaving under their arms and things like that, but in spite of it, not bad looking. They seemed to be anxious to appear sullen and tough, but they weren't too convincing."[21] It rarely happens that an interview with a male political group evaluates the men's looks.

The Women's Liberation Movement and the Media

Until a few years ago, scholarly works on the role status of women in American history fell into two categories. The first consisted of only two books —Eleanor Flexner's *Century of Struggle* (Camb.Mass,1959) and Andrew Sinclair's *The Better Half* (N.Y.,1965)—both broad surveys and both about as good as the paucity of the specialized knowledge at their disposal allowed. By far the majority of works in this field fell into the second category; biographies of important women and minute acts of activities of suffragists in various states. The biographical approach is not accidentally the most popular; nor is it accidental that almost all these works are by women. Most men . . . (and here I might add women) think of the women's rights movement as the demand by neurotic females to be like men. With a few exceptions only women have seen fit to write about the lives of women leaders, and these biographies, while they give the lie to the stereotype, are rarely accorded by male historians a respectable place in historical literature and are hardly ever mentioned in bibliographies appended to books that deal with the times in which these women affected history.[22]

Some feminists don't wish to deal with the media at all. Others argue that the only way to make women's rights a mass movement is to reach millions of women.

Almost all the major magazines and certainly all political, literary and radical periodicals have reported on the sudden rise of the new feminism. The question that troubles feminists is how to get publicity without being molded by the desire to make headlines and without being completely misrepresented, which has already happened several times.

Women have suggested a blacklist of reporters and periodicals that give distorted coverage of feminist affairs; that women speak only to women reporters and be photographed only by women photographers; that groups research the previous work of a writer to discover her biases before granting interviews and, furthermore, that they interview the reporter beforehand to learn what sort of theme she's been ordered to fit the interview to. Most importantly of all, feminists suggest that women demand the right to approve the final versions of copy and pictures before they are printed. Too often the media editorialized by publishing only pictures of feminists in unattractive poses or facial expressions.

The media editorialize coverage of WL activities in other subtle ways. *The New York Times* indexed an article about the WL Movement—"Desire for total equality"—under the Fashions and Home section of the paper. *Life* Magazine's article on the women's movement ended opposite an advertisement showing a muddled, incompetent woman driver running over her husband's suitcase *twice.*

The worst offenders in this belittlement of all women, and particularly of feminists, have been the news organs of the New Left and the underground press.

"Let them eat cock," a remark made by a Berkeley radical about the Bay Area WL groups, and the attitude it expresses, has been graphically realized in nearly every issue of the underground press.

Another interesting phenomenon is the book world's sudden realization that feminism will be one of the major movements of the seventies. A veritable cornucopia of book contracts has been offered to women in the movement. Marylin Bender has remarked on the irony in the fact that "the book publishing industry which has always underpaid, underrated and underemployed the second sex, should now be gallantly courting the Women's Liberation Movement."[22]

Literature and Vocabulary of the Women's Liberation Movement

"Women must learn the meaning of rage, the rhetoric of invective," said Marlene Dixon.

"We are damaged—we women, we oppressed, we disinherited. There are very few who are not damaged, and they rule . . . The oppressed trust those who rule more than they trust themselves because self-contempt emerges from powerlessness . . . We are damaged and we have the right to hate and have contempt and to kill and to scream. But for what? . . . Do we want the oppressor to admit he is wrong, to withdraw his misuse of us? He is only too happy to admit guilt—then do noth-

137

ing but try to exercise the new thought . . . that does not make up for what I have lost, what I never had.

"Nothing will compensate for the incomparable harm it has done to my sisters . . . How could we settle for anything remotely less, even take a crumb in the meantime less, than total annihilation of a system which systematically destroys half its people. . . ."

The collective thinking that is characteristic of the feminist movement is built on the feeling of identity with all women that consciousness-raising gives. In the preceding quote from Roxanne Dunbar notice the switch from "I" to "We." This interpenetration of identity is typcal of WL writing. As oppressed people living always in atomic home units, women have not been accustomed to working in concert; only lately have they realized again the necessity of organization if they are to make inroads on the intolerance that oppresses them. One woman's life is all women's life. In our society women of all classes and all races are oppressed by the demand that they be attractive and pleasing and make men feel good. The continuity of feminist experience gives energy to the cry: "Free our sisters! Free ourselves!"

> Our history has been stolen from us. Our heroes died in childbirth, from peritonitis; of overwork, of oppression, of bottled-up rage. Our geniuses were never taught to read or write. We must invent a history adequate to our ambitions. We must create a future adequate to our needs.

The literature of feminism abounds with newly realized injustices. It ranges in tone and control from the eloquent and moving poster quoted above to the vernacular of "You smug ugly rich man—you show your cherished power so easily, evoking fear with the glint of your eye and snap of your fingers. You love the women —those women who have learned out of fear to submit to your whims and desires. Those women who dress for you, chatter, laugh and cry for you."[24] Elizabeth Fisher stated that she began *Aphra,* the feminist magazine, out of "reasoned rage."

Here is another example of the rhetoric-and-the-agony common to feminist articles in the underground press. The difficulty is the monotony of the intensity. Entire pieces are written on the same high-pitched note. There is a tendency to cram a piece with adjectives the better to stimulate intensity.

> Women are the real Left. We are rising, powerful in our unclean bodies; bright glowing mad in our inferior brains; wild hair flying, wild eyes staring, wild voices keening; undaunted by blood we who hemorrhage every twenty-eight days; laughing at our own beauty we who have lost our sense of humor; mourning for all each precious one of us might have been in this one living time-place had she not been born a woman; stuffing fingers into our mouths to stop the screams of fear and hate and pity for men we have loved and love still; tears in our eyes and bitterness in our mouths for children we couldn't have, or couldn't *not* have, or didn't want, or didn't want *yet*, or wanted and had in this place and this time of horror. We are rising with a fury older and potentially greater than any force in history, and this time we will be free or no one will survive. Power to all the people or to none. All the way down, this time.[25]

America's mass media language is not yet furnished with the words for women's liberation. Woman is still the woe added to man. Everything must be redefined; women must muster the power that comes from forming original words that can both talk about the inner experiences of real depersonalization and that also can conjure the power that comes with forming original words "and with them, new ways of combining the cosmic net of forces."

The specialized vocabulary at use presently in the movement is psychologically confining, adapted as it is from black, New Left, and hippie argot. Its word patterns are so set that only stereotyped feelings are discussed. Rarely is there the inrush of feeling that occurs from a newly realized insight. Women meet for consciousness-raising to get to the *gut feeling* that all of them share. They speak to the question of sexism or male chauvinism. *Movement men* exercise *cock privilege* by relegating all the *shitwork* to *chicks*. When a *sister raps* about her oppression as a sex *object,* her sisters may still say, "Right on!"

A sister is unlikely to work a straight job. Poor and frequently hungry sisters *rip off* food and clothing from capitalist store owners who steal the labor of their employees.

A sister who doesn't understand that we are all oppressed by the humiliation of our sisters may be denounced as *anti-woman*. Sister are *fucked over* by a male-dominated society. Sisters who resist their oppression may be termed castrators by their oppressors. The *life-styles* of sisters vary. Their general goal is to *radicalize* the consciousness of women outside the movement through consciousness-raising actions.

While sisters can only imagine who they can become when they end their oppression, they are most *uppity* about the sex roles they refuse to inhabit. Sisters seldom make love but often fuck. Sisters are not "mindless commercial boob-girlies," nor are they toys, pets or mascots. They refuse to enter "lily-white racist" beauty contests. Sisters demand of the cosmetic industry: "Can make-up cover the wounds of our oppression?" Sisters are manipulated people, frightened and hurt by the reactions of a society that they sometimes delight to provoke.

The Women's Liberation Movement has been critical of the binds that its turgid vocabulary puts on women's ability to communicate with other women. Carol Hanisch wrote:

There is a great need for clarity in our language as in our actions. The leaflet that was distributed as a press release and as a flyer at the action was too long, too wordy, too complex, too hippy-yippee campy. Instead of an 'in' phrase like 'Racism with Roses' (I still don't know exactly what that means), we could have just called the pageant RACIST and everybody would have understood our opposition on that point. If we are going to reach masses of women we must give up all the 'in-talk' of the New Left/Hippie movements—at least when we're talking in public. (Yes, even the word FUCK.) We can use simple language (*real* language) that everyone from Queens to Iowa will understand and not misunderstand.

Chapter 4

Problems of 19th-Century Feminism

The struggle for women's emancipation has always been inspirited by the dialectic of whichever evolutionary and radical ideas were current. American feminism has linked itself with each protest against inequities and found in the struggle the material for its own movement. This self-discovery through working for others, this borrowing of ideas, tactics, and philosophical underpinnings from the male movements of the time has prevented the steady application of radical analysis to the question of women's oppression. In the end, women have found that the causes in which they fought so valiantly have each in their turn left women without the means of achieving full equality. Women never achieved the right to do and be whatever they pleased because even their protest movements evolved through working for others, through self-effacement in the drive to achieve human rights for whatever group was then considered most downtrodden. The attempts to operate from a mode radically individualistic and self-centered in its concentration on women's rights were fragmentary and never perceived as the *sine qua non* for female emancipation.

It was the churches that first taught women a dynamic for freeing themselves by teaching them to protest. "Protestantism, by its very nature, cannot set limits to the protests of its believers. The United States was both Protestant and republican and Michel Chevalier noticed: 'Protestantism, republicanism, and individuality are all one.' This ideal was bound to inspire women to protest, once they had learned not to organize against the fact of their inequality."[1]

142

When Northern American women in the 1830's began to organize to free the slaves, they learned the politics of agitation for human rights. The Grimke sisters were Southern abolitionists who came North to preach and lecture about the sufferings of the slaves. They were the first women to speak in public before male and female audiences. No one reform can occur by itself. In the process of speaking out against slavery the Grimke sisters had to fight for women's right to address the public. The Grimke sisters declared that "whatsoever it is morally right for a man to do it is morally right for a woman to do."

"The famous Pastoral Letter of the Congregational Churches of Massachusetts against the Grimkes was remarkable in its failure. It stirred up ten feminists such as Lucy Stone, for each one that it deterred . . . The Letter may have deplored the mistaken 'conduct of those who encourage females to bear an obtrusive and ostentatious part in measures of reform'; but that conduct had been the conduct of many Congregational Ministers, who were grateful enough for the funds and free work from women in their churches . . . It was revivalist preachers who had borrowed many of the shock tactics of the old Puritans and had taught women how to use them."

"In seeking to free the slaves radical women became conscious of their own lack of freedom. Through helping others, they learned to help themselves. The destiny of American women and American Negroes has been interacting, and still is."[1a]

The dangers of learning how to struggle for oneself in the course of struggling for others is that one may not develop the independent analysis which is the only way that women will ever effect the radical changes necessary for their emancipation. At some point women must learn to distinguish their interest and politics from those of the causes in which they are enlisted. They must comprehend the solitary nature of their oppression. The abolitionists in fighting for the rights of slaves did not realize that all women were united as an oppressed class. The analogy they did form between marriage and slavery was helpful for giving them insight into their oppression but it did not equip them with the political analysis and the strategy to free themselves. "In an extreme or moderate form, the arguments over the equality of the slaves were applied by some educated women in their marriages . . . The white man could be matched by his wife or his slave; the mother was the equal of the father; no human being should be the master of another. Those women who wanted to become equal with white men found themselves in the struggle for the slaves' equality with white men. The support of him became the support of themselves." History was to prove that the support of the slave was not the support of the woman. True radicalism inheres in seeking the causes of one's own oppression and rooting these out. When the female suffragists saw that black men had got the vote while they were still disenfranchised, many of them turned their backs on the racial inequities in America. The fact was that there had been two separate struggles all along. If American feminists had kept an awareness of the distinctive character of their own oppression, they would not later have proved such untrustworthy supporters of racial equality.

It was their sense of betrayal at the admittance of the black man to suffrage that led feminists to make the split in their movement that was eventually to narrow the struggle for the emancipation to the single issue of woman's suffrage. This narrowing of the focus of feminism, with its eventual rejection of a radical analysis of the position of women, meant that feminism could never get to the root causes of women's oppression. The result was that the full emancipation of women has yet to be achieved.

By the early nineteenth century, women and many free Negroes had lost the few political rights

144

which they had once had. These rights had only existed fleetingly because of the nasty and egalitarian fervor of revolutionary times. The considered laws of the nation and the states restricted the vote to free, white, male, property-owning citizens.[2]

Throughout the decades of struggle for women's rights, feminists changed their demands from higher education to access to the professions to the vote, but the underlying demand was always for autonomy. From the Seneca Falls Convention in 1848 on, women demanded the right to engage in public affairs. Elizabeth Cady Stanton, one of the organizers of the Convention, and Lucy Stone at that time espoused a radical form of feminism which if carried through would probably have led to the full emancipation of women. Both Lucy Stone and Elizabeth Cady Stanton were impelled into feminist activities by their anger at the wrongs that women suffered in marriage.

Elizabeth Cady's father was a judge. As a child, she spent hours crouched in the corner of her father's office, listening to the people who came to him with their legal problems. Many were wives and daughters of farmers; often the husbands had disposed of their small property, or taken their earnings for drink, or, in the event of a separation, had the sole right of guardianship of the children. Judge Cady was kind, and often dipped into his own pocket to help the women; but he reiterated patiently and endlessly that they had no legal redress, and his daughter was marked for life by that knowledge.[3]

Both Lucy Stone and Elizabeth Cady Stanton would have been comfortable in a women's liberation gathering because they insisted that the woman's body was under her own control whatever rights the law gave her husband in marriage. "Beginning in 1848, it was possible for women who rebelled against the circumstances of their lives, to know that they were not alone."[4] The feminists who launched the movement from Seneca Falls were strong in their belief that women were the equal and likeness of men except for their sexual differences.

As feminists gradually acquired the right to education and access to the professions, they focused on suffrage as a means of obliterating discrimination against women. All the early women's welfare programs were part of the fight for women's rights. Women needed special protection because they didn't exist as citizens. They were under the complete dominance of their fathers before marriage, and after marriage, they suffered a civil and political death. The law no longer regarded them as beings distinct from their husbands. The Temperance Union arose to safeguard women who had no legal redress against the abuses of alcoholic husbands. Feminist tracts moved from the expression of generalized unhappiness with the artificial limitations on women's activities to the demand for specific changes in customs and laws.[5]

In half a century anti-feminist arguments against woman suffrage moved from the preservation of femininity and the home to the state's right to decide which of its citizens could vote.[6] The anti-suffragist arguments shifted because the feminists themselves "increasingly emphasized those grievances and demands that pertained to women's relations to the government. At last the chief stress was on securing married women's property laws and other attempts to wipe out legal inequities."[7] More and more the strategies for the protection of women centered on the vote.

Unfortunately the feminist argument for woman suffrage changed over the years. In the beginning feminists argued that women had the right to vote as citizens and human beings. Later they asked for the right to vote so that they could bring their moral influence on the affairs of the nation. Demand for autonomy had always been consistent with the distinction between men's and women's worlds, but the pre-Civil War feminists always argued against the sexual division of life.

Once the argument for suffrage was based on the superior faculties of women, feminists had actually accepted such a distinction. Feminists hoped to get the vote by using the Victorian belief that ladies were the angels in a human world, but they thereby engaged themselves to appear publicly only within the guise of traditional femininity.

One reason for this major strategical error of accepting a world divided into men's and women's spheres was the anger and fear of the feminists on discovering that post-Civil War America was far from ready to enfranchise women. Women were shocked to discover that they had so miscalculated the tolerance of the nation.

The Fourteenth Amendment to the Constitution which federalized the exclusion of women from the vote was a traumatic blow which rigidified feminist thinking and made the women willing to make compromises that would have been unacceptable to them until then. The opinion throughout the North among their former allies, the abolitionists, was that the black man's suffrage would be endangered if accompanied by a request for woman suffrage. This was unacceptable to the radical feminists even though it was a correct reading of the nation's political temper. The republican state of Kansas rejected in 1867 a referendum that would have given the vote to women as well as blacks.

The sentiment of the country was completely intolerant of the vote for women. "The anti-suffrage cohorts went on conjuring hideous visions of an Amazonian sex pitted against 'man' . . . The basic argument on which the philosophy was grounded was that women *should* not vote or hold office because they *could* not. Here, too, the living record to the contrary in the growing total of suffrage states was either ignored or willfully distorted."[8]

Lucy Stone was able to reconcile herself because she accepted the abolitionists' claim that black men had suffered more than white women and that their cause must come first. She and Stanton and Susan Anthony joined the Equal Rights Association, a coalition of abolitionists, Boston intellectuals, and feminists. Stanton and Anthony became increasingly embittered after the passage of the Fifteenth Amendment. They ascribed the failure of the Equal Rights Association to back immediate woman suffrage to the preponderance of men in the organization. In May, 1869, they broke off from the men and women in the Association to found the National Woman's Suffrage Association which was absolute in its quest for immediate woman suffrage along with other social reforms. The Stanton-Anthony feminists were ready to ally themselves with anyone who was in favor of woman suffrage.

The weekly paper that they put out was a reflection of the broad reforms that the women demanded. NWSA (The National Woman's Suffrage Association) declared that marriage reform "is of more vital consequence to woman's welfare, reaches down to a deeper depth in woman's heart and more thoroughly constitutes the core of the woman's movement, than any such superficial and fragmentary question as woman's suffrage." At the same time Susan Anthony asserted that disenfranchisement was the major block to female emancipation. This dual stand on the nature of needed reforms confused other women. If marriage reform and the burden of domesticity was the heart of the woman question (which history has indeed shown to be the case) why need Stanton-Anthony secede from the Equal Rights Association over the question of immediate woman suffrage? *Revolution,* which was edited by Stanton and managed by Anthony, did give the movement a forum and direction, but the problem was that it pointed in all directions at once.

The NWSA acquired the habit of using quite contradictory arguments if both supported woman suffrage. *Revolution* is to be praised for keeping alive the radical tradition of feminism when the general trend was toward a more conservative approach.

In November, 1869, AWSA (The American Woman Suffrage Association) was formed in Cleveland and headed by Lucy Stone. It spoke for the growing population of women entering the professions and interested in getting more social freedom. These women were not yet ready to speak out for woman suffrage, nor did they make any radical analysis of the social structure. The schism between the National and the American was one between radical and conservative. The National regarded women's rights as a broad cause extending from political to social to sexual restructuring of women's identity. The American, unlike Susan Anthony, was interested in organizing working women and avoided issues that it considered might alienate the influential sectors of the community. Significantly *The Woman's Journal,* organ of the American, was a success in the decade that lay ahead while *Revolution* failed. This was indicative of the increasing conservatism of American society. By 1875 Susan Anthony had regressed to the Victorian issue of women's morality in arguing for woman suffrage in her article *Social Purity.*

The National had made another error by cutting itself off from the labor unions. In her anxiety to get work for women printers, Anthony sent them in as strike-breakers to union shops. After that she was no longer welcome at labor conventions.

The decade from 1880-1890 saw the suffrage movement turn conservative as a reflection of the lessening of social tolerance for militance. "The middle class was learning to identify organized labor with social turmoil." The strikes during the depression 1873-1878 "did not help to reassure women taught by press and pulpit to identify any kind of militancy with radicalism."[9] By 1890, the radical and conservative wings of the feminist movement had become reconciled. The National and the American merged to become the National American Woman Suffrage League which became the League of Women Voters in 1920.

In a period that saw the ascendancy of middle-class values, and in which feminism was cut off from labor, feminists ceased to ask radical questions. With the exception of Stanton, Charlotte Perkins Gilman and a few others, the movement chose to see the basis for female emancipation in systematic and legal attempts to convince the nation to give women the vote. The social makeup of the suffrage leadership was changing perceptibly. "There were fewer housewives or women who did the greater part of their own work and more professionals, writers, and women of substantial means." "The kind of day-to-day contact that had enabled Miss Anthony to organize Working Women's Associations and had sent her to conventions of the National Labor Unions had vanished." Feminism turned respectable and middle class in its ideas and goals as well as in its membership. "Another generation of women leaders was developing in this new atmosphere even while veterans like Miss Anthony, Mrs. Stone and Mrs. Stanton were still on the scene. The younger women were not, for the most part, distinguished by the breadth of their social views."[10]

Sympathy and rapport with the working woman were missing from Rachel Foster Avery, Carrie Chapman Catt or Harriet Taylor Upton who led the later stages of the fight for suffrage.

"Around 1900 the promise of the American Revolution in terms of human equality and liberty were forgotten in the effort to win the vote for a limited number of white Anglo-Saxon women."[11]

Unfortunately the women who did go among the poor did not apply a radical analysis to the causes of the oppression they found there. The women active in the social reform movement were also articulate suffragists but their orientation was very different from that

150

of the early radical feminists. At the beginning of the 20th century, many of the worst disabilities of American women had been eliminated and others, greatly reduced. "While many of the changes which had taken place had been the outcome of sharply fought legislative battles, in general, they reflected the continuing expansion of women's interests and their activities in industry, in business, and in the professions . . . the 1890 census listed 4,005,532 (women) as gainfully employed . . . in 1910 7,444,787."[12] It should have been evident to thoughtful feminists that the basic oppression of women was domestic, not legal or political, and that it was marriage and the family itself that generated their inequities. But many things militated against this understanding.

Society had changed its consciousness of social evils and how to deal with them. Whereas an earlier generation had been abolitionists, the society from 1880 on became social reformers. Institutional arteriosclerosis set in in post-Civil War America and radical change was discredited. Rapid industrialization had made some men rich and had made desperate the lives of their employees. As people became aware of increased social tension due to the acute contrasts between the rich and the poor, they institutionalized philanthropy and social reforms to help the poor. Feminists, rather than establishing their own ethics and inventing an analysis that would be productive of equality for them, went with the tide, and divided their energies between social reform and the suffrage movement. If women thought that suffrage would emancipate them they were only in agreement with their times.

Increased leisure had given the conscientious middle and upper class the time to idealize progress. Men and women came to believe that an educated public, if given the vote, could cure all social ills. Society was infinitely perfectable. To women, suffrage was a symbol of the equality necessary to effect reforms; this was the link between the feminists and the progressives.

"As noted earlier, the feminists were for the most part, middle-class women who, on every other subject" (except woman suffrage) "shared men's opinions. In that period, politics was the great national pastime; especially during the Progressive period, the feminists shared the widespread conviction that many social evils could be cured and sweeping social reforms effected by legislation. To the suffragists, the ballot was an instrument of actual power."[13]

In an age committed to reform through the system, the feminists did not think of making radical changes in their milieu itself. Feminists no longer asked radical questions because America would not tolerate them. The age one lives in determines the questions one asks and the forms of change one thinks possible. "The chief feature of social feminism was that it created roles for women that militated against their emancipation. Their benevolent enterprises met women's desires for useful and satisfying work without touching the sources of their inequality."[14] Social reform accommodated women's need to act without requiring them to move outside the prevailing definition of a woman's nature. All the arguments of the anti-feminists were based on the idea of the lady. Once suffragists urged female enfranchisement on the grounds of woman's peculiar spirituality and probity, they had moved back inside the enclosure of womanly concerns. It was possible to see social reform and philanthropy as pure extensions of the duties of the good housewife.

The suffragists and the progressives made the same miscalculation, that the vote of the majority of the people would cure most of the ills of society, because most people would vote for the good, their belief in democracy made them also believe that the reform of the techniques of representation would mean the reform of the nation. They underestimated the cleverness of professional politicians in manipulating the new techniques and the new voters, and they overestimated the ability of those techniques and voters to judge well and do good.[15]

The founding of the National Women's Trade Union League in 1903 fused educated middle-class women and working women for a common effort on behalf of working women. Settlement housework met the subjective needs of middle-class women because it showed that the social concerns of free women would not disrupt the existing order. American women never succeeded in thinking themselves out of the stereotype of marriage and children. Margaret D. Robins was perhaps the most important woman in establishing a contact between working women and the suffragists. She later broke with feminists over the Equal-Rights Amendment to the Constitution because even though it would (if passed) make women eligible for the higher-paying jobs reserved for men, it would repeal many of the protective laws for women workers that Mrs. Robins had helped to institute. Mrs. Robins, though recognizing a link between feminism and social reform, was more concerned with protecting the poor than with the achievements of full equality for women.

Middle-class reformers wanted to better working conditions with the help of union leaders, but they did not want to alter the basic structure of society. In their view, women would be free to enjoy what they should earn; even the socialists wanted to keep the factory system; they thought wrongly that, if working women owned the factory, they would feel more free when they worked within it. Only the anarchists wanted to put an end to factories, as far as possible, and to free women from

153

work, motherhood, the home, and all the chains of society.

The moderate reformers were successful because, in the first two decades of this century, they had the support of many Americans. Factory work remained a casual affair for most of the female sex; a woman's trade union seemed silly to the prospective wife, who hoped to rise in the world with the right sort of husband.

The militant feminists failed to make women hate men. The militant socialists failed to make women hate ladies. The sex war, like the class war, never became a popular concept in America, although both concepts were widely discussed . . . There was only gradual reform in the factories, and the gift of the vote to all adult women.[16]

The failure of feminism was the failure of American society to institute forms or analysis that would realize the promise of democracy for all Americans. The Declaration of Independence would never have been signed by any of the legislators in America from the Civil War to the present. All efforts for the emancipation of women have coalesced in periods of intense social ferment and public debate. While this is probably true of all movements for equality, it has been the bane of the feminist movement precisely because women are in the habit of adopting the attitudes, with only a few alterations for fit, of the predominant male culture. As a result, feminists have always eventually accepted philosophical and political ideas and demonstrations that have not been germane to their own emancipation. Women have not been self-centered enough to effect their emancipation.

It was the talent of the Progressive movement to use the diplomacy of Julia Howe and Frances Willard to persuade middle-class ladies in city and town to support social reform and woman suffrage, in order to save the home. Women had saved the morals of men and children within the house; now they must do so without.[17]

The resulting social feminists felt that the issue of woman suffrage would wait or did not think it essential to their high moral cause. The hard-core feminists, almost as far from true emancipation, believed that woman suffrage was essential to the success of all other reforms. Florence Kelley was a lifelong socialist but she had largely rejected the formulas of socialism for the Progressive doctrines that were the mainstream of the American ethos before the war. "Her whole strategy seems to have been based on the assumption that by organizing women and inspring them with a higher social consciousness before they gained the vote, it would be possible to lead them to final victory afterward."[18]

In this strategy she was a woman of her time—a Progressive social feminist. Her failure was the failure of the era to redefine society, politics and psychology to devise a strategy for female emancipation and working-class liberation.

The cyclical nature of the problem of the feminist movement is perhaps the most frightening conclusion that can be drawn from an examination of feminism in America. The suggestion that housework be professionalized and the same supporting arguments were presented at the recent New York Congress to Unite Women. Contemporary feminist literature repeats often Engel's dictum that within the family the husband is the bourgeois and the wife, the proletariat. The necessity of repeating the same arguments over and over again suggests the intractable, irrational nature of the opposition to feminism. Men remain the humans, women, their female creatures only capable of continuing in the never-diminishing round of domestic duties to which they have been relegated.

Charlotte Perkins Gilman was one of the few feminists to attack the cult of domesticity. William O'Neill, author of a book on the decline of feminism, criticizes Charlotte Gilman and Florence Kelley for not embracing socialism as the only system that could emancipate women through removing the burden of housework and child-rearing to the public domain. Yet at the turn of the century socialism seemed a long-range ideal, rather than a pragmatic means of redressing social ills. There was not then, as there is now, the example of successful socialism in other countries. Gilman wanted to lift the burden of domesticity from women but her failure to provide the social context in which this could be achieved is simply the measure of resistance in America to any collective solution to the problems of family life.

Inequality of the sexes still exists because the family structure has remained basically unchanged. Unless a middle-class feminist is prepared to challenge that family structure head-on, contemporary feminism will perhaps revert to the form of the earliest feminist—the generalized urge toward individual autonomy—before feminists concentrated in winning a long list of specific rights which they assumed would add up to autonomy.

Many tracts written between the Civil War and World War I either called for or predicted the machinization and professionalization of homemaking chores . . . They assumed that once women had won the right to work beyond the domestic sphere they would automatically do so, if only they could be freed from household drudgery. Cooperative kitchens and other such arrangements would give them the freedom and enable them to find remunerative careers suited to their individual tastes, while those women (and men) with talent and liking for housework would become skilled, well-paid professionals doing jobs hitherto done by housewives who, in many cases, had neither talent nor liking for the work.

Obviously the inferior position of women was somehow associated with the isolation of each family from every other family and with the sex-determined division of labor within the family.[19]

Charlotte Gilman knew that it was the popular conception of the family that was the obstacle to full sexual equality. Our present economy is dependent on women as a reserve for cheap labor. The labor of women is cheap because they do not believe their work is important to the economy. They have accepted the popular idea that women only work to get luxuries for their families.

Without quite realizing it, we have come to depend on a work force of married women who do not think of themselves as workers and are not treated seriously on the job. Only when we look back in history do we see how they have been pulled into wage work and pushed back home at the convenience of the changing economy. Women make no noisome ghettos, join no unions, organize no demonstrations, come when they are called, and go quietly when they are bidden.[20]

To succeed, feminism must obliterate this cherished and carefully nurtured media-image.

The mistakes of Anna Shaw, who replaced Susan Anthony as leader of the movement upon Anthony's death, should be learned by every contemporary feminist. Anna Shaw was limited by her geographical and sociological background from making the alliances that would have given feminism some much needed strength. Anna Shaw "remained too much the rural Westerner to understand the need of combining with urban progressive and labor forces to win over the

Eastern cities. She could only understand the need of working with the evangelical churches and temperance women of the small Western towns, and here woman suffrage was successful." Shaw failed to broaden the base for the movement because she limited herself to the public with which she was most comfortable. There is some danger of this deliberate delimitation of membership in the new feminism. The WLM is presently urban or college-centered in its program and in its attempts to reach the public precisely because that is the expected basis of its membership. To succeed, feminism must engage the sympathies of the small-town woman and of the churchgoing housewife. The WLM must not remain an organization of professionals, intellectuals, and radical students.

During Shaw's leadership of the movement, Southern delegates had gained a remarkable ascendancy. She alienated the Easterners raised in the anti-slavery tradition by accepting Southern vice-presidents in the organization. "As one Negro leader wrote to another about the suffragists, 'All of them are mortally afraid of the South, and if they could get the Suffrage Amendment through without enfranchising coloured women, they would do it in a moment.' "[21]

The final stages of the suffrage movement are tarnished by the compromises that suffragists made to win backing for the vote. In the North much of the resistance to the vote was based on the idea that the new immigrant women voters would provide natural material for the corrupt machine vote in the large cities. The race question in the North actually meant prejudice against the Irish, Italian and Jewish immigrants. To manipulate this racial fear to the advantage of woman suffrage, Northern suffrage leaders began to urge the advantages of the "educated vote." Even Elizabeth Cady Stanton declared in 1902 that "suffragists would be willing to restrict the vote to educated women provided only that the insurmountable qualification of sex be forever removed."[22]

The final leader of the suffragists was a new breed of Westerner. Carrie Chapman Catt was the new professional woman, diplomatic, and politic and shrewd . . . She could manipulate the politics necessary for legal change and the details necessary for social change without committing herself to enmities . . .

Anna Shaw, with her evangelical ideas and vocabulary, had been unable to communicate with her educated professional women and the union organizers of the cities. This failure had led to the revolt of the Eastern cities from the control of the Western and small-town mind . . . The new and Militant Woman's Party . . . was modelled on the example of England where the militants were organized and powerful.[23]

The Woman's Party was a coalition of Harriet Stanton Blatch, daughter of Elizabeth Cady Stanton, and Alice Paul, both of whom had lived in England and realized the effectiveness of the militant feminists there. The period from 1896 to 1910 is generally considered least active in the history of the early feminist movement. Harriet Stanton Blatch returned from England in 1910 to find no effort being made to persuade Congress to vote in woman suffrage and a complete lack of political knowledge in the movement. The by-law of feminism at that time was to educate the public, but there was no active work going on. Blatch formed the Equality League, which initiated the practice of suffragist parades. These parades riveted public attention on the feminist cause.

Alice Paul formed the Congressional Union, which utilized militant tactics to push for a Federal amendment on woman suffrage. She revitalized the feminist movement, but she was excluded from leadership and replaced by Carrie Chapman Catt, who had the political finesse and deviousness to organize the final drive for woman suffrage. The amalgamation of the Equality League with the Congressional Union was called the Woman's Party.

Led by the indomitable Alice Paul, the Woman's Party continued the fight for female emancipation long after it was a dead issue to the rest of America. It was the Woman's Party that initiated the drive in 1923 for an Equal-Rights Amendment to the Constitution. Forty-seven years have gone and the Amendment is still not passed. It is presently supported by NOW and was introduced in this session of Congress by Senator Eugene McCarthy and Senator John Tower, Representatives Catherine May and Martha Griffiths. The amendment reads: "Equality of rights under the law shall not be denied or abridged by the United States or by any state on account of sex." The Amendment has been held up in every Congress by the Senate subcommittee on Constitutional Amendments. After Congressional approval the Amendment would require approval by three-fourths of the state legislatures.

The new vitality of the Eastern suffrage leadership was another sign that the savagery of slum conditions had moved the frontier of civilization back from the settled towns of the West to the line between tenement and middle-class suburb in the cities . . . Progressive Reform had to deal with the city jungle as well as the subsistence farm.

The shifting of the focus of reform activity back to the Eastern city came just at the time that the suffrage movement needed to conquer the Eastern states.

In the history of woman's search for the freedoms of the body and of the mind and of the spirit in America, nothing had aided her more than the advance of technology and urbanization. Her quest for liberty has been interacting with the spread of an industrial civilization across a continent.[24]

160

Lillian Wald, Margaret D. Robins, and Jane Addams went into the slums to persuade working women of their need for suffrage. Andrew Sinclair sees the support of the working women for suffrage as crucial to its attainment. Ella Bloor, a middle-class labor organizer, made better working conditions her priority; suffragists made the vote theirs. Bloor said: "For many of the secure middle-class ladies, the suffrage movement was a mere feminist fad. I tried to make them see the really vital importance of suffrage to the working women, as a weapon against economic insecurity. And I tried to make them see that not the vote alone was important, but its proper use in building a better society.

"Once women did get the vote, political differences split the labor leaders from the middle-class suffragists." In Ella Bloor's opinion, the splendid and militant Woman's Party degenerated to a 'narrow, anti-labor sect.' In fact, most of its members had nearly reverted to the American middle-class idea of what freedom and equality meant, the opportunity to become a lady.[25]

For a brief period before ww I, feminism was quite a stylish movement, but with the death of progressivism, it was no longer popular. When Roosevelt and the Republican Party disassociated themselves from the idea of progressive reform, the ideals of social reform were discredited. This early demise suggests that pre-ww I feminism was indeed a fad and that the women were for the most part only inspired by the ideas and politics of the men then in control.

Political and legal reforms did not bring women economic equality. "After the war, employers avoided equal pay laws by simply refusing to give women men's jobs."[26] The women who had earned their Ph.D's before the war discovered in the 20's that they could not advance in their careers. Fewer women went on to graduate schools and women lost interest in careers as opposed to mere jobs.

The flappers of the 20's thought of self-fulfillment through exploration of the new social and sexual mores. They looked to marriage and domesticity rather than to economic independence for their major satisfaction in life. The identity of women in America was basically unchanged. Women made no demands for an enlarged social role.

Those women in the 30's who did pursue careers did so at the conscious expense of their private lives. A constellation of authorities from Havelock Ellis, Freud, and God told women and men a woman's happiness was in her home and family life. Women stopped asking who they were and what they wanted. They accepted the old Victorian redefinitions of womanhood.

"The double standard of morals did not mean simply that men enjoyed sexual advantages denied to women, but also that masculine activities were self-justifying while women had always to identify themselves with the highest moral and social good to excuse even relatively modest enterprises." The practical result of this was that two generations of mothers told their daughters that the most important thing in a woman's life before her marriage is her chastity, after her marriage, it is her husband and children.

The reverberations of these teachings may be seen in the uneasiness that women radicals feel at concentrating on women's issues and at calling themselves feminists. An evaluation of the problems of American feminism makes evident that women must engage in a self-initiated radical analysis of their social identities and the options that our society and polity offer them. Women must recreate their cultural tradition and rediscover the myths of the female. Our culture now is entirely male in its symbols and in the priority it gives them, in its determination of what is and is not natural.

Western society has mechanisms for utilizing the expression of male alienation—the academic and criminal worlds—but no institutions exist that will unequivocally foster the talents of an eccentric woman or provide emotional support for the needs of a free woman. A girl growing up has no models for womanhood. Womanhood is an unknown, a hole in space. Men are the humans, women, the aliens, an afterthought of creation.

The creation of a vital feminist movement depends on women's revival of self-knowledge, unqualified by men. They must create a female principle in order to create a politics. Politics is the expression of the needs of the recognized self, and women have been denied self-knowledge for thousands of years.

In order to do this women will have to fight.

> The right of a man to support, protect, and defend (i.e., possess a family.) This notion has led the Black movement onto a path, already trod by the white working class. That is, among the demands of Black radicals is the right to 'family.' The system agrees. Every major magazine and television special pronounces the virtues of family and the tragedy of the Black man's inability to get one in his economic situation. And though Black radicals oppose Moynihan and his Report, they agree with his thesis: The Plight of the Negro *Man*. Get your manhood; get a Black woman, put her in a house, breed her, then you will be a man, just like the white man. And Kathleen Cleaver tells the *San Francisco Chronicle* reporter that she wants nothing more than a private life as a mother and housewife; that she is only fighting to help her man out, so he can be a good father and breadwinner . . . Indeed poor Black women have to emerge before the movement will move toward real liberation."

The new domesticity and demure womanhood— black women get behind your man—both physically and psychologically, is cited as undeniable example of the way that the feminine role has been constructed by men to support the male identity. This has required millenniums of self-denial. The black male's reassertion of female submission is a clear indication of the basis of manhood in our society. The men are black and proud; the women are black and pregnant. This is simply a less subtle statement of the usual relationship that obtains between men and women in our society.

It's time for women to reject the masculine definition of themselves. Women have just got to learn how to be free.

Chapter 5

Nineteenth-Century Feminism and WLM as Different Phases Same Movement

Feminists in both the early and contemporary stages of the movement for women's emancipation have been typified as unnatural. Their detractors have delighted to picture them as thin-lipped, man-hating, frustrated, neurotic malcontents.

Formerly any advocacy of sexual pleasure outside the bounds of marriage, or for purposes other than procreation, gave fuel to those who would damn the women's movement. Nowadays anti-feminists are more subtle and possibly unaware of their anti-feminism. Men hail the liberated woman as one free and eager to engage in promiscuous sex and to explore the newly discovered sexual superiority of women. This vision of the liberated woman as a promiscuous radical is but a variation on the Victorian vision of women as animals, completely defined by their physical natures.

Eventually suffragists demanded the vote to extend the aegis of their moral superiority—used to order the home—to the nation, which was badly in need of social and moral reform. It was the earlier phase's failure to focus on the family as prison that doomed female emancipation and necessitated the rebirth of the movement.

While radical feminists in the WLM articulate the desire to annihilate sex roles, the family and homelife as we know it, almost all feminists continue to live with men or carry on relationships within the old framework. There is as yet no evidence of a radical rejection of home and children as the main goals of the adult female.

Hard-core 19th-century feminists and the social feminists of the Progressive Era both rejected Marxism. Charlotte Perkins Gilman, one of the most gifted intellectuals in the last generation of the early feminists, was both a socialist and a feminist, but she did not think of using socialist institutions (day-care centers, paid maternity leave) to free women of the domestic burdens that she had pinpointed as the barrier to female emancipation. Social feminists moved from socialist doctrines to bourgeois reform social work because they saw socialism as a long-range program while they wanted to act immediately to aid the poor.

Today's radical feminists are wary of hard-core socialists and of the New Left who see women's liberation as a step toward releasing more fighters for the struggle for the liberation of the oppressed classes. Yet feminists are actively pressing for the inception of socialist institutions as the prerequisites to the emancipation of women.

The early feminist movement pressed for autonomy at first to do whatever they chose, but later they asked for autonomy within their own sphere—the enrichment of the cultural, spiritual and moral life of the homes of the nation. Early feminists constantly denied that women would unite against men and vote in blocks for their sex interests, and history proved them right. Social feminists, like the Progressives, of which they were one manifestation, wanted to maintain power, stability and order while redressing the imbalance of class distinctions and economic differences. No levelers, they saw progress as individual freedom and abhorred collective domination.

Today feminists are arguing that all women must unite to end their oppression by men. NOW of course simply wants women to share in the power that men have. Radical feminists want to eliminate sexual class, economic and racial distinctions, which are the bases

166

for power and domination. Radical feminists are practicing the elimination of power within their own organizations by seeking to remain leaderless. They rotate officerships and divide creative and repetitive work by lot. The mainstream of the WLM is gradually using this allotment of offices by rotation because the equality issue has become a major plank of contemporary feminism.

Early feminists wanted and had leaders in plenty. Women with great natural abilities rose in the movement through the application of their gifts to women's issues. Women today feel that the idea of leadership, and of a hierarchy with gradations of prestige, is a facsimile of the world of domination of one species over another and of man over nature.

This leaves unsolved the problem of individual achievement in the fulfillment of women's talents. Some women are bound to attract more interest and acclaim than others. One restriction suggested and applied in some groups of WLM has been for gifted women to use their talents as resources for the group and for aiding their sisters to develop equal proficiency. This tactic forbids women from engaging in activities and achievements in organizations not concerned with WLM.

One direct parallel in both stages of the feminist movement has been the middle-class composition of their memberships. In the early phase, this led to preoccupation with middle-class goals and a failure to seek ties with working women whose support was necessary to achieve suffrage. Their middle-class membership also meant that the feminists allied themselves with reformism and maintaining the status quo.

Contemporary feminism is likewise middle and upper middle class in its membership and preoccupations. The present campaign for the right to abortion on demand has been pressed by articulate, educated women as the constitutional right of women to control their own bodies and regulate their own sex lives. Sociologists have found that sexual mores have undergone the most change among the college-educated middle- and upper-middle class women.

Another example of the bourgeois orientation of the WLM is the focus of the demand for equal opportunities for hiring and advancement. Generally this pressure is being applied to the institutions that employ college-educated women. Professional women who wanted to rise in the business world formed NOW, the forerunner of WLM. College graduates are every year swelling the ranks of discontented workers who resent not being able to advance according to their educated abilities and also resent having to choose between marriage and career. No such alternatives exist for working-class women.

At the recent Congress to Unite Women held in New York, some of the few black women in the audience complained that too many of the workshops focused on the problems of educated women. Throughout the Women's Liberation Movement just as it existed throughout the first phase of feminism, there is an assumption of middle-class goals and middle-class sophistication about sexual roles. In fact these goals and the sophistication that are and have been taken for granted in the past only come with the distance that college education gives from the round of domestic drudgery and babies.

Even though radical feminists declare that all women must unite to end domination, WLM has not made attempts to answer the needs of minority and working-class women any more than 19th-century feminism did. The realization that the movement must appeal to women of all socio-economic classes and races is still only intellectual. It remains an idea that appears now and then in position papers.

The argument that minority women prefer their ethnic organizations for the solution of their particular problems is similar to the initial relinquishment of Irish and Jewish immigrant women to socialism and militancy and disguises the same antagonism.

Feminists at one point suggested a restrictive suffrage that would enfranchise middle-class women while disenfranchising most foreigners . . . Suffragists moved from the democratic idea of suffrage for all citizens as just to the racist use of fear of the "ignorant vote" of the immigrants. They mirrored middle-class American fears of the immigrants.

The Women's Liberation Movement is still in its egalitarian stage, but, as noted above, it is an imperfectly practiced egalitarianism that has not broken down class and racial barriers to unite all women. *Feminae Caveant*. At present there seems little danger of WLM making the concessions to expediency that the suffrage movement made after the Stanton-Anthony group broke off in embittered rage from the Equal-Rights Association. Perhaps feminism now is stronger than it was before. Time moves faster. While the early feminists worked for more than thirty years in the abolitionist movement without distinguishing the issue of women's rights from that of the emancipation of the slaves, the radical students of contemporary feminism worked only a few years in the civil rights movement before they were made to realize that fighting for black civil rights was perhaps an escape from their own oppression as women.

Best of all, a few coalition actions with the New Left have disillusioned many feminists about the nature of their support from male groups. There may be no expedient concessions this time.

Footnotes

Preface

1. R. D. Laing, *The Politics of Experience* (New York, 1967), p. 190

Chapter 1

1. *Mademoiselle*, February, 1970, p. 287
2. *Ibid.*
3. *Ibid.*
4. Janine Sade, "The History of the Equality Issue in the Contemporary Women's Movement"
5. The FEMINISTS—"History of the FEMINISTS"
6. Jessica Furie, "The Lot System as a Fundamental of the Feminist Movement"
7. Sade. *op. cit.*
8. Pamela Kearon, "Rules and Responsibility in a Leaderless Revolutionary (Feminist) Group"
9. Carol Hanisch, "A Critique of the Miss America Protest"
10. *Us* (New York, October, 1969), pp. 113-115
11. WOMEN: *A Journal of Liberation,* Vol. 1, no. 2, inter., 1970, p. 67
12. *Ibid.*, pp. 72-75

Chapter 2

1. *Lay My Burden Down,* ed. B.A. Botkin, p. 55
2. Andrew Sinclair, *The Better Half* (New York, 1965), p. 43
3. *Ibid.*, p. 46
4. *The Report of The President's Commission on the Status of Women* (New York, 1965), p. 227
5. Calvin C. Hernton, *Sex and Racism in America* (New York, 1965), p. 167
6. *Ibid.*, p. 168

7. E. Franklin Frazier, *The Negro Family in the United States* (Chicago, 1939), p. 125
8. Hernton, *op. cit.,* p. 162
9. *Ibid.,* p. 144
10. *Ibid.,* pp. 83-84
11. *Ibid.,* pp. 135-136
12. *Botkin,* ed., *op. cit.,* pp. 59-107
13. *Look,* 9/23/69, p. 77

Chapter 3

1. H. Eckstein-Diener, *Mothers and Amazons: the First Feminine History of Culture* (New York, 1965), pp. 281-283
2. *Ibid.,* p. viii
3. *Ibid.,* p. 172, 47
4. *Ibid.,* p. 287
5. Caroline Lund, *The Young Socialist,* 12/69, pp. 9-10
6. Evelyn Reed, *Problems of Women's Liberation* (New York, Merit Publishers), p. 43
7. *Ibid.,* pp. 20-21
8. *Life,* 7/12/69, pp. 48ff
9. *Bulletin,* 1/12/70, p. 12
10. Richard Schickel, *The Stars* (New York, 1962), p. 176
11. *No More Fun & Games,* Issue Three, pp. 26-27
12. New York *Times Magazine,* 1/25/70, pp. 88ff
13. *Ibid.*
14. "Abortion Counseling Information," distributed by NOW and NYLAR (New York, February, 1970)
15. New York *Times Magazine, op. cit.,* pp. 98-99
16. *No More Fun & Games, op. cit.,* pp. 25-26
17. Judith Brown, Part II of *Towards a Female Liberation Movement* (Boston), p. 28
18. New York *Post,* 11/26/69
19. New York *Times Magazine,* 2/9/69, p.85ff
20. *The Daily News,* 1/29/70
21. *Philadelphia,* 10/69
22. Aileen Kraditor, *Up From the Pedestal* (New York, 1968), p. 5

23. New York *Times Book Review,* 3/9/70
24. Lisa Leghorn
25. *Rat,* 2/6-2/23, p. 7

Chapter 4

1. Sinclair, *op. cit.,* pp. 39ff
2. *Ibid.,* p. 31
3. Eleanor Flexner, *Century of Struggle* (Camb., Mass., 1959), pp. 72-73
4. *Ibid.,* p. 77
5. Kraditor, *op. cit.,* p. 27
6. Flexner, *op. cit.,* p. 309
7. Kraditor, *op. cit.,* p. 181
8. Flexner, *op. cit.,* p. 143
9. *Ibid.,* p. 153
10. *Ibid.,* pp. 217-219
11. Sinclair, *op. cit.,* p. 299
12. Flexner, *op. cit.,* p. 230
13. Kraditor, *op. cit.,* p. 19
14. William O'Neill, *Everyone Was Brave* (Chicago, 1969), p. 143
15. Sinclair, *op. cit.,* p. 316
16. *Ibid.,* pp. 314-315
17. *Ibid.,* p. 318
18. O'Neill, *op. cit.,* p. 239
19. Kraditor, *op. cit.,* pp. 22-24
20. Caroline Bird with Sara Welles Briller, *Born Female* (New York, 1968), p. 38
21. Sinclair, *op. cit.,* p. 298
22. *Ibid.,* p. 299
23. *Ibid.,* p. 201
24. *Ibid.,* pp. 201-203
25. *Ibid.,* p. 312
26. Bird, *op. cit.,* p. 30
27. Roxanne Dunbar, *Female Liberation as the Basis for Social Revolution* (Boston, New England Free Press), p. 3

Guide to Literature of the WLM

Lucinda Cisler has compiled a bibliography of literature on the movement available from her at 102 W. 108 St., N.Y. 10024. The New England Free Press has a list of over 20 articles on WL. Their free catalogue can be obtained by writing to NEFP, 791 Tremont Street, Boston, Mass. 02118. Some of the newsletters put out by the movement are *Women's Monthly* put out by MEDIA WOMEN—Media Women, Box 1592, New York 10001.

> BREAD AND ROSES *Newsletter*—Newsletter, Box 116, Cambridge, Mass. 02138.
>
> *Tooth and Nail*—Bay Area WL, c/o Wesley Foundation, 1398 Bancroft Way, Berkeley, Calif. 94704.
>
> *Off the Pedestal*—Bay Area WL, 376 Addison St., Palo Alto, Calif. 94301.

Among the journals being published are:

> WOMEN: *A Journal of Liberation*—$2.25 per issue—3011 Guilford Ave., Baltimore, Md. 21218.
>
> APHRA: *Free Women, Thinking, Doing, Being*—(feminist literary pieces)—Box 355, Springtown, Pa. 18081—$1/issue.
>
> *No More Fun & Games*—Female Liberation, 371 Somerville Ave., Somerville, Mass.

Notes from the First Year: collection of papers from early WL *group*—$1 from REDSTOCKINGS, 799 Broadway, Rm. 412, N.Y. 10003.

LILITH: *Journal of Women's Liberation*—Women's Majority Union, Box 1895, Seattle, Wash. 98111.

Bibliography

Bender, Marylin: *The Beautiful People,* New York, 1967

Bird, Caroline with Briller, Sara Welles: *Born Female,* New York, 1968

Blake, Judith: *Demographic Science and the Redirection of Population Policy,* Berkeley and Los Angeles, 1966

Brown, Norman O.: *Love's Body,* New York, 1966

deRham, Edith: *The Love Fraud,* New York, 1965

Dunbar, Roxanne: *Female Liberation as the Basis for Social Revolution,* Boston (New England Free Press)

Eckstein-Diener, H.: *Mothers and Amazons,* New York, 1965

Farber, Seymour and Wilson, Roger, eds: *The Challenge to Women,* New York, 1966

Flexner, Eleanor: *Century of Struggle,* Cambridge, Mass., 1959

Hays, H.R.: *The Dangerous Sex,* New York, 1964

Hottel, Althea K., ed.: *Women Around the World,* vol. 375, The Annals of the American Academy of Political and Social Science, Philadelphia, 1968

Jones, Beverly and Brown, Judith: *Towards a Female Liberation Movement,* Boston, 1968

Jordan, Joan: *The Place of American Women,* Seattle, Wash., 1968

Kraditor, Aileen S.: *Up From the Pedestal,* New York, 1968

Laing, R.D.: *The Politics of Experience,* New York, 1967

Ludovici, L.J.: *The Final Inequality*, New York, 1965

Marcuse, Herbert: *Eros and Civilization*, New York, 1955

Marx, Engels, Lenin, and Stalin: *The Woman Question*, New York, 1951

Masters, William H. and Johnson, Virginia E.: *Human Sexual Response*, Boston, 1966

Mead, Margaret and Kaplan, Frances Bagley, eds.: *American Women*, The Report of the President's Commission on The Status of Women, New York, 1965

Mitchell, Juliet: *The Longest Revolution*, 1966 (*New Left Review*)

NEW YORK RADICAL WOMEN: NOTES From the *First Year*, 1968

O'Neill, William: *Everyone Was Brave*, Chicago, 1969

Rainwater, Lee with Weinstein, Carol Kane: *And the Poor Get Children*, Chicago, 1960

Reed, Evelyn: *Problems of Women's Liberation*, New York, 1969

Rieff, Philip: *Freud: The Mind of the Moralist*, New York, 1959

Sinclair, Andrew: *The Better Half*, New York, 1965